MW01520522

The Ledge and The Abyss:

Near Death, Rescue, and The Search for Meaning

Dean Waggenspack

Rosaleen Waggenspack

Make Moments Matter

Dean Wagg

www.BelvoirPress.com

www.belvoirpress.com

www.TheLedgeBook.com

Cover Design by Megan Lewis

Website design by Xponex.com

Book Trailer by Terry at www.TriLevelRecords.com

Softback ISBN: 979-8-9877396-1-7

First Edition

Dedication

To Karl, Devron, Ben, Jason, and Malik. Your bravery on the rocks is a testament to the greatness of the human spirit. We will be eternally grateful for your service in our time of need.

To the Command Center, especially Daniel, thank you for being a source of strength when it was needed on the 911 call. Your decision to send the helicopter was so critical.

To Travis, Billy, Beau, and Curren. Your professionalism and teamwork on the helicopter are a source of inspiration. You embody "Semper Paratus".

To everyone at the Gov. Juan F. Luis Hospital in St. Croix who served us so well, thanks for your patience and your care. We will especially never forget Cadira, Dr. Lauren, Amanda, Steve, Grace, Amber, and Kristen.

Table of Contents

Introduction

"As long as there is life, there is hope", Bjarne Mamen, assistant typographer on the Karluk, stranded in the Arctic Sea, December 1913

"Where am I? How did I end up here?"

Those were the thoughts running through my head on November 22nd, 2022, when I was pulled underwater and into a cavern with no light and no way for me to escape. Shortly after, I thought about how my wife and son would think they'd seen me die, and how after a long, drawn-out process, they would be right.

The Ledge and the Abyss is the story of that day and its aftermath. None of us knew when we woke up that morning that it would be a life-defining day. But the events about to unfold would form a tale of incredible bravery, miracles large and small, and the power of the will to survive.

It is not just a story about one person. This book is a celebration of people and their capacity to do good. All of us have the choice to consciously and diligently use our talents when the moment asks for it. The rescuers' and healthcare professionals' skills and humanity shine a bright light on what we can be as a community.

This event and its aftermath could have taken my life, but didn't. The search for meaning and purpose, and the growth that has come from my reflections, has been an important part of the journey since that day.

This story is, as one friend put it, "An Incredible story of resilience, hope, and bravery. Throw in some faith and luck."

Key Characters in Rescue and Recovery

Waggenspack Family

Dean Waggenspack, and Rosaleen (Rose) Waggenspack

Stephen Waggenspack, oldest son, present at the tide pools

Courtney Waggenspack, daughter

Nathan Waggenspack, middle son

Amanda Waggenspack, daughter-in-law

Luke Waggenspack, youngest son

The Rescuers

John and Amie Jarvie, made the initial 911 call

Karl Frederick, Tan Tan Tours driver and first person on site

Devron Smith, Tan Tan Tours driver and second person on site

Ben Torkelson, first Rescue St. Croix Volunteer on site

Jason Henry, second Rescue St. Croix Volunteer

Malik Garvey, firefighter and ambulance driver

Lishari-Shumba Bailey, firefighter

US Coast Guard Helicopter Crew

Lieutenant William "Travis" Cox, pilot

Lieutenant SG William "Billy" Boardman, co-pilot

Beau James, Jr, aviation maintenance technician

Curren Hinote, AST (aka rescue swimmer)

US Coast Guard Command Center

Daniel Capestany, Command Center Command Duty Officer

Keren Gabriela Zepeda, Command Center

Health Care Professionals

Dr. Lauren Bacon, primary ER Doctor

Cadira McIntosh, ER Nurse

Amanda Crossland, ER Respiratory Therapist

Doctors Lacey Menkinsmith and Beth Joseph

Dr Delareoux, ICU Doctor

Steve Chmura, Wednesday day ICU nurse

Grace Kim, ICU respiratory therapist

Amber Wyse, Wednesday night ICU nurse

Kristen Lee, Thursday and Friday day ICU nurse

NEAR

DEATH

Chapter 1: The Fall in St. Croix

"This thing that happened to me, it happened for me" Ted Lasso season 3, episode 6

It all started with a great idea.

With four adult children plus a daughter-in-law, we rarely have family vacations together anymore. We decided that Thanksgiving 2022 was going to be a family vacation in St. Croix. It was an opportunity to get us all together for some fun. Rose set the wheels in motion in November 2021 by asking everyone to set aside time for this vacation the following year.

We picked St. Croix because most of us like the ocean and we wanted to be somewhere warm. As a US territory, passports would not be needed, simplifying travel.

The US Virgin Islands consist of St. Thomas, St. John, and St. Croix. Located in the Caribbean Sea, it was purchased in 1917, becoming part of the United States as a territory. St. Croix is about 1,200 miles southeast from Key West, Florida, about the same distance Washington DC is from Key West. It includes the easternmost point in the United States in the western hemisphere, Point Udall. Because of its location in the tropics, its temperature is mild year-round with the average temperature every month in the mid-80s to the mid-70s.

St. Croix is not very big; At 84 square miles, you could fit 20 St Croix in Rhode Island. The poverty rate is 40%, which is more than double the poverty rate of any US state. It's population of 50,601 (2022 census) is less than the population of the city I live in, Kettering, Ohio. It's a small place with a lot of beauty and great people.

Rose and I, and our oldest son, Stephen, all arrived on Monday, November 21 around 6:00 p.m. After a nice dinner, we went back to our house for rest. Getting up the next morning, Tuesday November 22, Rose and I walked the one mile to our local beach. We were there by ourselves enjoying the water and the rocky beach. As Rose recalled, "We just had a short time walking the beach and talking. What a nice start to our time here."

The three of us decided to check out the Annaly Bay / Carambola Tide Pools that morning, because we wanted to see how interesting it might be for the rest of the family, who were scheduled to arrive the following day.

The tide pools were an easy pick, because they show up on EVERY list of fun things to do in St. Croix.

A tide pool is much like a wading pool, except it is part of the ocean. Black, irregularly-shaped, jagged volcanic rock creates the walls of the tide pool sheltering it for the most part from the waves. On a typical day, the volcanic rock walls are 6-10 feet above the sea level, especially on the ocean side, thus holding back most of the waves. Because the rock is porous, water seeps in and out, thus refreshing the pool with cool water from the ocean. With a water depth that varies from a few inches to a few feet, an individual can lounge in the water. It is a nice place to relax, enjoy the ocean water, and be relatively protected from the surf.

Formed long ago, there are multiple tide pools, separated by jagged rock walls where the lava flowed farther out into the sea and then hardened. Climbing from one pool to the next is as simple as climbing out of a swimming pool.

An article I read noted a few things to be careful about:

> *"As far as precautions, you'll want to go at low tide and with favorable sea conditions. While much of the trail is shaded, the tide pools and beach typically are not; be sure to wear lots of sun protection.*
>
> *There are no amenities, so bring plenty of water and a snack.*
>
> *Since the terrain is rocky and uneven, wear sturdy footwear that ties or straps onto your feet.*
>
> *For your safety, do not hike alone, and proceed only if you are physically fit enough to complete a hike safely.*
>
> *There is little to no cellphone reception along the trail, service in this area is spotty at best.*

Vehicles can be parked at Carambola Beach Resort from which you can walk to the trailhead.

Do not leave any valuables in your car while hiking"

At the time, that felt like an exhaustive list of "things to be careful about". But it did not mention one item that would soon become an important part of the story, which is the impact trade winds can have on the waves.

There are two ways to get to the tide pools. One way is to hire a jeep with a guide from a tour group. The other is to hike a well marked 2-mile trail on your own through the rainforest. A chance to be in a rainforest? Why not take the hike? That was an easy choice for us.

We parked near the Carambola Resort entrance and began our hike. The path was often narrow, but that made it easy to follow. It was muggy and warm early that morning, but the path was shaded and the terrain was not too difficult.

As usual, Rose took the lead walking, she walks fast all of the time. Stephen and I stopped a couple times to take in the views of the forest and the ocean. Soon, we could not see Rose and both of us hoped the path was easily discernible. It was. As we got to the crescent-shaped beach, we finally caught up to Rose.

One of the precautions was to go during low tide since that's when the waves were the smallest. On Tuesday, November 22, 2022, low tide was at 11:41 a.m. We arrived at the beach at almost that exact time. For the three of us, it was an easy hike winding through the forest.

We arrived at the beach and could see that we'd have to climb over rocks to get to the tidal pools. It is a short, 200-yard scramble to the first tide pool. We were happy that when we arrived at the tide pools, we only saw two other people there. We'd get to explore the place almost on our own.

We briefly talked with two other people in tide pool #1. They were on a cruise and this was a side trip they made while visiting St. Croix.

Rose, Stephen, and I decided to do a little more exploring. We climbed out of the first pool and continued west (away from the beach) over the short wall to pool #2.

The two people, who we learned were John and Amie Jarvie, later told us they had explored that second pool a few minutes earlier. Amie, the more adventurous of the two, wanted to walk around in it for a while. John was not feeling comfortable about the pool and convinced her to go back to tide pool #1.

We walked past them and climbed over the small wall separating the two pools. In the northeastern most corner of the second pool, we saw a small hole (we called it a "drain hole") that looked to be about the size of a volleyball in width. It had a swirling motion formed by the water as it filled and then emptied. We mentioned to stay away from that hole because we might slip into it and twist an ankle or stumble on it and hurt ourselves on the sharp rocks. We got as far away from it as possible.

The second pool was not very big, about 50 feet long in an east/west direction and 30 feet wide north/south. We moved to the far western end of the second pool where Stephen and I stepped down into the water. Most of the time, the water level was less than waist deep. At one point, I asked Rose to join me on a rock in the pool for a picture. Stephen had to the gone farthest west end of the tide pool to see what was over the next wall (another tide pool). We gave Stephen Rose's phone, on a lanyard with a waterproof clear pouch to take our picture. Stephen took a picture of Rose and I enjoying our vacation.

After a couple more minutes laying around the pool and exploring it, Stephen said, "let's head back." Rose got back up on the wall on the ocean side of the tide pool. I said, "I'll be right there. I want to check out this crevice in the cliff." The shore side of this second tide pool was a rock cliff approximately 50 feet high. There was one spot with a large crack in it. I decided to check it out. Stephen was walking behind me. I was 30 feet from Rose, who was on the volcanic rock wall, with her back to the ocean.

I was walking in water no more than shin deep, as close to shore as possible. I did not have my back to the ocean. None of those precautions mattered, because Mother Nature had a different idea.

It was about 12:25 p.m. We'd been at the pools for about 40 minutes. In a moment, the water level got significantly higher, the result of an unseen wave crashing over the rock wall with a tremendous force and violence. The waves must have been 10 feet high to breach the rock wall creating the tide pool.

Miraculously, Rose was in a spot where the waves did not knock her off the wall into the tide pool.

The first swell knocked me down and spun me around. If you have ever been knocked over by waves in the ocean, you know the power of the water and the disconcerting feeling of being tossed about. You lose all perspective of up-and-down and what direction you were heading. After getting knocked down, I surfaced in-between the first and second swells. I was confused and hollered out to Rose that I lost my glasses, hat, watch, and shoes. Those were the last words Rose heard from me.

* * * *

Rose was watching the tide pool from the top of the ocean-side rock wall. She wasn't in the water and did not feel the power of it surging. Water that was 18 inches deep was now 4+ feet deep. She thought, "we were in this enclosed tidal pool. It will calm down in a moment or two. We will wonder, what was that?"

Rose saw me pulled by the water towards the rock wall, right in front of her. From her vantage point, I did not reach out; In fact, she could not see my arms because they were under this surging, boiling water. She saw my face out of the water looking up at her, but she did not sense any panic. All-of-a-sudden, my face disappeared. For a moment, she stood staring at the spot and questioning, "He's gone? Maybe the water is so deep that he is underwater?"

Frozen by the suddenness of events, she kept staring at the water, expecting me to reappear, though there was no shadow of my body under the surface.

Stephen was knocked over by the same sudden surge of water as I. He saw me, about ten feet in front of him and to his right, also get knocked over.

"I momentarily regained my balance, in a different part of the tide pool than I was a few seconds before," he recalled. "A second surge of water did the same thing to me and brought me right below where my mom was standing on the rock wall above. Rising up after stopping my momentum by planting my feet against a rock, I saw my mom pointing a few feet in front of me and saying, "He's gone. He was right there, but he's gone. He was down there".

Somehow Stephen had instinctively braced himself and could get a sense of what was going on. The water was very frothy, almost angry-looking and more than 4 feet deep. Since we were in the corner of the pool, in that moment he thought I had hit my head on the walls and was underwater.

Instinctively, Stephen lunged to where Rose said she last saw me, frantically flailing under the water's surface to try to find or feel for me. He was reacting, trying to grab a limb, any part of my body. The water was moving so much, he could not see below the surface.

He had no way of knowing that he could never reach me, but he had put his own body into the dangerous spot mine had been.

"All of a sudden, a third blast of water hit me. Immediately, I was sucked down into what felt like a hole," Stephen recalled. "Probably because I was standing up when the third surge came, I had a moment to spread out my arms and legs to make myself wider. I felt myself rapidly being sucked underwater. I pressed my arms and legs against anything I could feel in order to stop the sinking. My entire body was in a hole and the water was at least a foot above my head. I gasped and held my breath. The water was pouring over me, it was going around me, and completely filling the structure I was in. It felt like I was in a tube, but completely immersed in water."

"The water was relentless in pulling me down. It felt like I was in a vacuum getting sucked downward. I thought for sure I was about to get sucked to my death. I could feel my legs banging against rocks on each side of me as I searched for a foothold. My elbows and shoulders scraped against rock as I struggled to stay up; the water fought to send me down."

"At that moment, I 100% thought I was going down to my death. I was going to drown."

Rose saw the third swell of water hit Stephen, who began to disappear downward just like what she had witnessed with me. In her mind, it all happened so fast, she could not react. Stephen was rapidly sinking feet-first right in front of her eyes. Then, he too was gone.

The water subsided and Stephen's head appeared above the churning surf. He had a moment to catch his breath and try to climb out of the hole. Before he can react further, another surge of water, coming from behind him, started tugging him down the hole again. Stephen called out to Rose, who could see the fear in his eyes.

He looked up at her and said, "Mom, if you don't help me, I'm gonna die."

Until she heard his voice, Rose, in her state of shock, didn't realize Stephen was in danger. She remembers, "His words kicked me into action. I went into 'momma bear' mode. I instinctively reached my arms down to him from my place a few feet above him on the rocks. We grabbed onto each other's arms. I braced my legs as the water tried to tug him under again into an abyss that I could not see. I was so numb I did not recognize the force of the water nor did I truly understand what was going on. All I knew was I was holding onto my son's arms as we fought against the water. Miraculously, I did not get pulled off the wall into the water with him."

As the water stopped flowing momentarily, Rose straightened her legs, lifting Stephen a little bit out of the water. That effort was enough for Stephen to free himself. He scrambled onto the wall, covered in blood from scratches on his legs. The two of them hugged each other, adrenalin flowing through their bodies and their minds yet still very confused about what had happened in the last minute.

Stephen was thinking, "Now that I made it out of the hole, I'm in a complete flight or fight state of mind. I am reeling. What just happened to me? How I am still alive? The water kept crashing. I asked my mom again where dad was."

Briefly, the two of them could see the hole in the floor of the tide pool again. Rose said to Stephen, "Dad couldn't have gone down that hole." Stephen answered, "I was going to be sucked down it, so yeah, he could." That explained why they could not see or feel me.

Now Rose understood what had happened. I had been sucked down that hole. She started screaming for me along with Stephen, "Dean (Dad), are you there? Can you hear us?"

They screamed into the water and into the wall for about 10 minutes. They were met by silence, except for the rushing in and out of the water.

Chapter 2: Down in The Hole

There've been times in my life

I've been wonderin' why.

Still, somehow, I believed we'd always survive

Now, I'm not so sure

You're waiting here, one good reason to try

From *This is It* by Kenny Loggins and Michael McDonald

The second wave threw me down the hole. I distinctly remember the sickening sound like being flushed down a drain. It was like a "thunk" sound as I was forced underwater. The hole was similar to a continually running drain. The drain filled when the swells of water filled the tide pool and then emptied as the water returned to the ocean. It was as if I was riding a fast-moving water slide, unable to control any movement.

The third wave deposited me in a place I can best describe as a pitch-black closet with a pocket of space where I could breathe. There was no light, only darkness. There I was, trapped in the darkest place you can imagine with water up to my armpits, no idea where I was and no idea how to get out.

Gathering myself, I realized I was standing on a small ledge of rock. I could tell that to my left it was a drop into the water, but I had no idea how far down.

Immediately, I yelled, "Rose, Stephen, I am here. Can you hear me?"

No response. I tried calling out to them again and again. "I am alive down here. Help me."

I waited to hear if there was any response. I experienced only silence and the water.

Fear began to set in quickly with the realization that no one knew where I was. Neither did I. The suddenness of the water pushing me around in the tide pool and then sending me downwards into this cavern in the ocean had thrown off my sense of direction. It was too dark to gain any clues of where I was compared to where I had been a few seconds before.

"How could they not hear me? Was I far away from them?" I thought. "Were they injured or trapped somewhere like I was?" It had happened so fast that I was totally confused.

I could not see the "ledge" I was standing on but I knew I was above the bottom of the ocean. To my immediate right was a column of rock. I grabbed tight to it, holding onto it as if my life depended on it. Having something solid to hold and lean into was the best I had.

I had no idea what was to my left. I sensed it was an abyss, filled with deeper water, but I was not going to find out. Immediately in front of me was a wall of rock. I didn't know what was behind me, but I sensed a wall of rock relatively close. The "ceiling" to this space was a couple feet above me. It was pitch black.

Occasionally, I could see a small hole in the rocks a couple feet above me and to my right that brought in fresh air. I wondered if that was a possible escape route. But it was too high up, too small for my body, and would fill with water most of the time. I knew this because I could not see light when it filled up.

I had no idea where I was in relation to where I had been a few minutes ago. Was I far away from Rose and Stephen? I did not even know which way I was facing. I estimated the space I was in was about the size of a walk-in closet. It was not very large; big enough for me to stand in and enough air space.

The water where I stood was at the level of my chest. The tide would bring more water into the space, causing me to swallow more salt water.

As those waves came in, they smashed me into the column of rock to my right, lifted me up and scraped me against the rock, and then bang my head on the ceiling. My body was getting badly cut up every wave. It hurt as if I was pushed against a wall by someone behind me. The air got knocked out of me. Each wave meant I was floating above the ledge. I wondered if I would land back down on the ledge or into deeper abyss. I had no idea what might happened next. I clung to the column of rock to my right, even though it hurt to be scraped against it. It represented stability, where everything else felt like it led to the bottom of the ocean.

Not hearing from Rose and Stephen, I soon realized I was alone. I stopped calling out to them.

I stood in my "grave" in the water with no idea how to get out. I was trapped in a place with no clear exit. Even if there was an exit, where did it lead to? More water? A deeper place in the ocean? More rock? My fate felt sealed. Time slowed down. I could see nothing but darkness and hear nothing but water. I was left with my thoughts.

I did not feel claustrophobic, even though I was trapped in a small, dark cavern. Although I was in a confined space, I did not have an irrational fear of the space. My location was, in a perverse way, my "safe" space. Although it was dark, cold, and foreboding, it was at least not totally immersed under water. Allowing claustrophobia to be a part of my thinking would have been a waste of energy.

My life did not pass before my eyes. Nor do I remember seeing a bright light. No angels appeared. I was present in the moment, feeling the water move around me, trying to figure out where I was relative to where I had been. I was not thinking about my past or my future. No "what ifs" or "what I would do later."

I was not pumping myself up thinking I was brave and strong for lasting that long. I was not congratulating myself in any way. I was hurting and getting colder every minute. Things were hopeless, but something in me kept me from giving up. Time and nature were going to settle my fate, but I was not going to give in.

Realistically, I had no hope. I did not think I was going to miraculously escape and reappear alive and well. During this time, I was doing one thing—existing in those rocks. Perhaps it was a survival instinct. I do know that I tried to steel myself for the next wave that was going to pound me. I knew the next wave would slam me against the sharp volcanic rock. As I struggled for balance and gasped for breath, I inadvertently swallowed more sea water.

Running through my mind was disappointment that my life was going to end this suddenly. How could something so pleasant, a walk to the beach, be turned on its head? It felt like a crazy, bizarre way to die. I thought *I still have a lot of things I want to accomplish in my life. Well, I guess those things are not going to happen.*

All I could think about was trying to assess my situation. I kept coming up with ideas of how I might escape, even though escape seemed impossible. I thought *I am in a pitch-black small cavern. No one knows I am alive. The waves knock me against the rocks, weakening me more. I don't see a situation where I am going to be rescued. Should I be thinking about how to rescue myself?*

Strangely, I don't ever remember giving up and thinking I should quit existing. Maybe that is how the subconscious mind works. As Bluto in *Animal House* said, "What! Over? Nothing is over until we decide it is." That quote did not come to me in the cavern, but it resonates now.

I was conscious of being truly present in the moment. Since the future was so bleak, that was not of concern. I don't remember my "life flashing before my eyes" meaning I was not thinking about the past. I was focused on the moment I was in, most of the time.

My mind cycled through four thoughts:

One: I cannot believe I am going to die today under these circumstances. No one would ever know about how lonely and hard it was. I was trapped with no way out in a place where the tide was starting to come up. Eventually there would be no air pocket to breathe.

Two: I can't believe my wife and son saw me die. How is seeing me disappear impacting them? Were they suffering? What might they be doing right now?

Three: Get prepared for another wave to come. It is going to make me colder. It will bash me against the rocks, increasing my pain. Be ready.

Four: What's the escape route? I don't know where I am. I don't even know which direction is towards shore. It is pitch dark in here, I cannot see the way out. Every breath was a gasp, as if I had run up a large flight of steps. Because I could not get my breathing under control, I knew I wouldn't make it far under water. If I decided to try an escape, I would only have one chance. Failure meant I would surely drown in the abyss.

It is weird to be thinking about the impossible—an escape. But it was all I had to cling to. That is why I characterize this time as a time of no hope, but not hopeless.

As time passed, I got colder because all I had on was my swim suit. My breathing got very shallow, the result of saltwater in my lungs. Calling out for help felt fruitless, but I tried a few more times.

"Is anyone there? Help me. I am alive." My voice got weaker from the strain and the cold.

Forty minutes of cold, dark, alone, battered, and baffled about how this had come to pass. I took no risks in the tide pool. I had so much more I wanted to accomplish in my life. I was still relatively young and in great health. I had races I still wanted to run and hikes I wanted to complete. My children were making their way through adulthood and I wanted to watch that happen. There were books I planned to write. Rose and I were thinking about what we would like to do special for our 40th Anniversary and beyond.

I grieved for myself and my family.

Chapter 3: He's Gone; What Do We Do Now?

"You never know what worse luck your bad luck has saved you from."
Cormac McCarthy, No Country for Old Men

While I remained in the cavern underwater, a lot was going on above the water's surface. While I struggled to stay alive, Rose and Stephen were trying to come to terms with what happened.

After my disappearance, Stephen and Rose kept screaming and frantically looking for me. No response. They were standing on the rock wall, yelling out in all directions, to the rocks, to the sea, in a circle. They had no idea what happened to me, other than I had disappeared down the hole, under the water, and had not surfaced again. Where was I in relation to where they were? Had I been swept 10 feet, 50 feet, 100 feet away? Had I hit my head and sunk to the bottom of the ocean?

"I was scared", Stephen recalled. "The water was still sloshing around a lot. It did not feel safe. I looked at Mom and I could see she was beside herself with dismay. Scared. Maybe in shock. I knew I needed to get her out of there. But I was fighting the flip side of not wanting to leave my dad. I looked over the wall into the first tide pool and saw John and Amie. I yelled to them; *my dad is gone!*"

Rose thought to call 911, remembering Stephen had her phone. But the phone was gone. It was on a lanyard but it had been ripped from Stephen's body while he was fighting not to be sucked underwater. It was gone forever. Her phone, like her husband, was lost in the abyss.

"Initially, I did not want to leave where I was standing. It was the last place I saw Dean." Rose recalled. "I asked Stephen to go to the first tide pool to see if the other couple, John and Amie, were still there and get them to call 911. After he made contact, Amie came back to help while John went to get his phone."

John went to get his phone to call 911. Amie stuck with Rose and Stephen to look for me. Not seeing me, they thought that with Stephen's experience in the water, I was sucked down the hole and maybe that hole led out to sea. The structure of the pools made it hard to see out into the ocean from their vantage point.

As time passed with no sound from me, Rose realized I had been underwater for a long time. She had been yelling and looking for 10 minutes. She began to recognize that her husband couldn't be alive. No one survives 10 minutes underwater.

Her body started to tremble. She knew she was in danger of panic and shock. She needed to get Stephen, John, and Amie out of there before she succumbed and was too weak.

"We have to head back to the beach. It isn't safe here," she told Stephen. He has since told Rose that he remembers being the one to say that. In the confusion of the moment, Rose remembers thinking, "Stephen would want me out of here, but would never ask it of me. I had to ask him to leave. He would only leave if I asked him to."

Who knows, maybe they both said, "We've got to leave, it's not safe." But neither of them heard the other because the circumstances were overwhelming.

"I momentarily thought about diving into the water on the outside of the pool to look for my dad," Stephen said. "I knew that was a dumb idea because the waves were crashing against the rocks, but I wanted to find dad."

They had a difficult decision to make: How much longer do they stay and call out for me? It was not safe on the rocks. However, once they made the decision to leave, that would be acknowledging I was dead.

"I could tell that mom was going into shock. She looked scared and had a distant look in her eyes," Stephen recalled. "I was afraid for her wellbeing. Would she even be able to make it back to the beach?"

Of our children, Stephen is by far the most like Rose. Like her, he is very extroverted. Rose tells people about Stephen that, "he came out of the womb shaking people's hands" and "on an extroversion scale of 1 to 10, Stephen is a 12". As a toddler, when we would go on a beach vacation, he would get to know the adults in houses by us. I can remember some saying, "we need to get his name; he is going to be President someday." At any social gathering, people will leave it knowing who Stephen is and probably think of him as a friend.

Stephen is super competitive and confident in his ability to get things done, as is Rose. Short in stature, he excelled at basketball through his aggressiveness, desire to win, and leadership abilities. He has an abundance of confidence in his own capabilities and his persuasive powers. He always seems to "recollect winning the family board games we played last Christmas" whether that was true or not.

All of his strengths were going to be needed in the next few hours.

Thinking that the most likely outcome was I had gone out to sea, helped them make up their minds to move off the rocks, return to the beach, and look out to sea. The four of them scrambled up the rock wall a few feet to look out to the ocean but did not see my body.

Ten minutes was probably long enough to know this was not going to end well. In addition, Rose's fear for the safety of the rest of them was growing by the moment. They decided to leave.

As they started back for the beach, they saw my Air Force Marathon hat floating in the water, headed out to sea.

That was the sign that solidified to Rose, "my husband is gone. It was gut wrenching to leave the spot where I had last seen my husband. Was I abandoning him? Might he be calling out to me right then and I had not heard? But my fear overwhelmed me, it was time to go."

The hike back to the beach was a time of reflection for Rose. "My rational brain knew Dean was dead. My heart prayed he had hit his head and was unconscious. I didn't want him to know he was dying. I didn't want to think of him being afraid. I had my first conscious prayer, *Please Lord, let him have hit his head so he didn't know he was dying.*"

"Had the two of us left anything unfinished between us?" she questioned. "Was there anything she wished we would have said to one another?" The immediate answer was, "No". Earlier, we had taken a walk together to a beach close to our VRBO before Stephen woke up. We enjoyed a walk on that beach, alone, and talking together. She thought, "He knows how much I love him and I know how much he loved me. We didn't leave anything unsaid." That knowledge comforted her in that moment. She felt herself steady and knew she was strong enough to make the hike back to the beach and wait for help to arrive.

"I don't know what I am going to do for the rest of my life without him," she thought, deep inside herself.

The return to the beach was a couple hundred feet. They retraced the steps they had taken with so much joy just an hour before. The climbing they had to do along the rocks felt a lot scarier than when they had gone out. Everyone was rattled as they clung to the rocks and worried every time a wave came crashing near them. Making it through that part, they started walking on the rocky shore away from those volcanic rocks.

* * * *

On the beach, John handed Rose his phone to talk to the 911 center. She gave them all the information she could (although she got my age wrong by one year). The four of them sat on the beach to wait.

John and Amie Jarvie were on a cruise of the Caribbean. November 22, 2022 was their one day in St. Croix. Like me, Amie had done a lot of research and the tide pools were their top priority. They had plans to visit the pools and then take in as much of the island as they could in their single day.

John is about 6'6" tall with a ready smile and a laid-back demeanor. Amie is definitely the planner and the more adventuresome of the two. Their first meeting is a fun story, like one out of a Hallmark movie. Amie's daughter lives two blocks from John and is in the same church. John and the daughter's husband worked together with the young men's group in the church. One day, the husband said, "My mother-in-law is moving out here (to Utah). You should date her.".

John's reaction was, 'No, I had gone through a rough divorce five years ago.' Finally, the kids arranged a dinner and to play some games at their house. John, agreed, saying, "Let's get it over with." The world had a different idea for him. As he said, "From that first day, we really hit it off. Very similar people. When we got married, four and a half years ago, we both made a promise to go on a honeymoon every month. We go somewhere all the time."

St. Croix was their "monthly honeymoon".

"I thought that (Dean) had been pulled out to sea," Amie recalled. "I remember asking if he was in good shape and could swim." She continued to look at the ocean for a sign of me.

A family of four from Atlanta hiked down to check out the tide pools. When they learned the story, they changed their minds about going to check out the pools. They stayed to be supportive. Rose and Stephen sat together, out in the sunshine, but their world was dark.

"I will never forget mom and I holding each other, crying at our loss," Stephen recalled. "Hearing my mom say, *I don't know what I am going to do without him* was really tough to hear. "

Stephen told me that there were two feelings he would never forget from that day. One is the feeling of the water sucking him down nearly to his death. Two is sitting on the beach hearing his mom say "I don't know what I am going to do without him" and being unable to do anything about it. "Her feeling of despair that her husband was gone was so strong."

Because of the shape of the beach and the tide pools, they could no longer see the spot where this had all happened. The loneliness of the next 30 minutes was the longest of Rose's and Stephen's lives.

The two held each other, to be there for each other. Now back on the safety of the beach, Rose knew that soon she would have to function. Her brain was ping ponging all around with thoughts of what she would need to do. Her heart was focused on what just happened and the memory of my face just before I disappeared. She questioned the reality of it all.

Stephen had his own thoughts to deal with. He knew his dad was underwater, dead.

He was a bundle of conflicting emotions. Confusion. Questioning what just happened. Anger. Frustration. Sadness. He thought, "We did not do anything wrong. We were not being stupid. We went at low tide. It was sunny and warm out. Beautiful, calm day. We saw that hole earlier. We did not think it was very big. But we actively said out loud to each other, let's get away from it. We will go to the other side of the pool. Out of nowhere these three waves come upon us and pull us to the hole we wanted to avoid." A wide range of emotions were going on inside him.

Rose was crying and said, "I just wanted to have a family vacation". She was feeling irrationally guilty that she brought us to St. Croix. But that is where her mind went as she sat on the beach crying.

At one point, Rose's brain broke through with thoughts of our other children arriving on flights the next day. She wondered, "Should we call them now? Should we tell them to come or not to come? Given what happened and how I "died", would the children want to come? She wanted to give them what they needed, but what would that be? Would my body would be recovered so they could see me one last time?

She asked Stephen, "Should we call the kids and tell them not to come?" He said simply, "I don't know Mom. Let's wait."

In that moment, not making a decision felt like the right decision. The two of them cut lonely figures sitting quietly, leaning on each other in that dark place on a sunny beach. Time no longer mattered, so she wasn't keeping track.

Rose was trying unsuccessfully to calm her brain and allow her heart to accept "I am a widow."

In her musings, she thought, *despite having perhaps the healthiest husband on the planet, I was a widow because of this crazy, unpredictable event. It made no sense. I struggled to fully accept what my eyes had seen and my brain rationally knew. Dean was gone. I was a widow. I was the one who wanted a family vacation. I was the one who picked St. Croix because of the VRBO I found. Guilt joined all the other emotions coursing through me. My inner world became darker.*

The time dragged on. Slowly

* * * *

Unnoticed initially by Rose, a flurry of activity was occurring down the beach away not far from where they were sitting.

A tour group arrived via three jeeps at around 12:55 p.m. The jeeps and their guides were bringing a few groups of people down for a guided tour of the tide pools and to have a fun afternoon. This happens every day at the tide pools, guided tours, a little partying, and learning a little about St. Croix.

The tour guides were totally unaware of the situation having shown up to do their job.

Luckily for us, the tours were led by guides Karl Frederick and Devron Smith, natives of St. Croix. Karl and Devron have intimate knowledge of the tide pools, having driven groups of people down to enjoy the pools hundreds of times.

Amie saw them arrive and recognized that they must be people who knew the area. She approached them to tell them what had happened.

Waking from her inner thoughts, Rose saw the tour groups and became nervous. She was horrified to think they would be soon climbing on the rocks and enjoying the water that was her husband's grave. She thought, "They can't go over there to the pools. No one should go into the tide pools today because they were dangerous."

Hearing the story, one of the tour guides (Rose learned his name was Karl), came running up to her. He urgently said, "Tell me which pool you were in, what you witnessed, and exactly where your husband disappeared". She explained the circumstances as best she could.

It was clear that Karl was very familiar with everything about the tide pools. As Rose described what happened and where it happened, Karl recognized the area. But in Rose's mind, since her husband had been gone about 35 minutes, what was the use? Nobody survives that.

Karl grabbed her shoulders, looked her straight in the eyes, and promised, "We will find him."

Karl took off running to the tidal pools with the other guide, Devron. Their mission was undoubtedly an impossibility. Rose yelled "be safe" after them. Karl and Devron bounced over the rocks "like mountain goats" Stephen said. They hurriedly made it out on the rocks.

* * * *

Rose and Stephen stayed on the beach waiting for the first responders to the 911 call to arrive.

"When Karl told Mom he was going to find dad, I was thinking that's kind and appreciated, but the hole is full of water, you are not going to find him," Stephen said. "Even if you do find him, he is dead." He knew it was hopeless.

As Stephen paced the beach with his mom, he was trying to hold her, but felt a rush of guilt. First, he had left his dad back in that terrible place. Second, these two strangers were out there trying to find his dad and he was not doing anything. He thought, "I am an able-bodied, healthy male. I can walk on some rocks and search for him. I would not let mom to go out there. I realized my place with my mom at this time."

Rose and Stephen sat disconsolate on the beach. The other people on the beach talked to them trying to get their minds on something else.

They noticed that a Coast Guard cutter boat had arrived north of the pools out in the ocean. Now they knew for sure that the 911 call was being responded to. But the boat remained far out to sea. They did not know if the cutter was going to do anything and had no way to communicate to them. Much to their frustration, they could not understand what was taking the EMTs so long.

Chapter 4: Making Contact

Hope... is the companion of power, and the mother of success; for who so hopes has within him the gift of miracles. Samuel Smiles

For Karl Frederick and Devron Smith, November 22 started as another normal day of work. As tour guides for Tan Tan Tours, they prepared to take small groups of tourists down to the tide pools for relaxation and fun in the warm water. Like most days, they jumped in their Jeeps and picked up their respective group of tourists who were ready for a good time. Karl had been doing tours for 15 years, so he knew the specifics of the tour. He took his customers through the safety features on the rough road to the tide pools and the procedures for their arrival. Along the journey, both of them used their knowledge of St. Croix to talk about the island's history.

Arriving at the beach, a distraught woman ran up to them cautioning them of a "dead man in the tide pools". The woman pointed out the dead man's family sitting not far away on the beach, waiting for the rescuers summoned by the 911 call to arrive. Karl and Devron were taken aback; they had heard of people who had died or been injured at the pools before. They had never experienced a drowning victim before. What were they to do?

So much for this being a normal day. Without hesitation, Karl walked over to the dead man's family to get the story. "I know the pools well. I asked the woman (who I learned was Rose) to tell me exactly where the disappearance happened," Karl said later. "I could see the loss on both of their faces. My heart was breaking for them. I knew I needed to help them, however I could. Once they told me they were in tide pool #2 and the hole, I knew the spot exactly. I told them we were going to find their missing person. I immediately ran to the pools."

Karl is tall, thin with a mustache and small goatee. He has a calm intensity about him, belying the laid-back demeanor of what you might imagine of a Caribbean Islander. Born in St. Croix, he has lived most of his life there. He took a detour for a few years as a master chef in Kennebunkport, Maine at the White Barn Inn and Resort preparing food for the wealthy and famous at that well-known location. The cold weather eventually drove him back to St. Croix. While most of Karl's family moved off the island after the closing of the large refinery in 2012, he stayed behind to be with his grandmother, who he characterized as the most important person in his world.

Devron is wiry, with a mustache, goatee, and close-cropped hair. Quiet and reserved by nature, he is also a native of St. Croix. Like Karl, he has been taking people to the pools for a long time.

Karl was first to arrive at the spot where he knew the hole was in tide pool #2. Unexpectedly, the water level in the tide pool was much deeper than normal. That confused him momentarily. Getting his bearings, he could see some water draining down where he knew the hole was, but he could not see the outline of the hole.

Nevertheless, he laid on his stomach next to the hole with water swirling around him as the tide came in and out. Sticking his face in the most likely place for the victim to be located, he yelled out, "Are you there? Can you hear me?"

No response.

Raising up slightly because the water was surging in, he realized that when the hole filled with water, sound wouldn't travel. He waited for the water to recede and stuck his head into the hole again to call out.

He tried again, "Are you there? Can you hear me?". To his surprise, he heard a response from a voice somewhere in the rocks, "I am here. Help me." He was stunned.

He turned to Devron, who was standing nearby, and asked, "Did you hear that voice?" Devron said he did not hear anything. Karl needed to get confirmation because he was not certain if he made up hearing the voice or it was real. He called again, this time with Devron standing closer, leaning in and listening intently. A response came back from the rocks; faint, but distinct, "I can hear you. I am alive. Help".

Devron looked at Karl with wild-eyed amazement. They both heard the voice. They had found me.

* * * *

I had been in the air pocket for about 40 minutes by this time. I was freezing cold. I could barely hold my breath for 2 seconds. I had swallowed a lot of salt water. As the waves came into my dark space, they continued to bang me against volcanic rock, ripping my skin. Then the surge of water lifted me off the ground to bang my head on the rocks above me. It has been a long time out here.

I had no idea what was going on above my sea grave. Rose and Stephen were on my mind. I had no idea if they were alive or not. I knew if they were alive, they were suffering because they had seen me die. I simply tried to endure the cold and the water.

Out of nowhere I hear, "Are you there? Can you hear me?"

I am stunned to hear a voice. It has been so long underwater that I was not expecting to hear anything. How could someone possibly find me? I had not been able to hear Rose and Stephen when I first went down. I was not attuned to listening for voices. Somehow, I heard him, whoever it was, calling out to me. I recognized that it was a real voice and responded immediately.

"I can hear you. I am alive. Help me." It took all my strength just to get those words out. They were the result of a weakened voice, but strong enough to carry to that voice calling out to me.

My world had just changed. Again.

My initial reaction to hearing this voice was a combination of relief, excitement, and apprehension. I was so tired and so weak. However, now my thinking switched to the importance of maintaining contact with this disembodied voice, my lifeline to the real world. I did not think I was "saved" by any stretch of the imagination. Could I dare hope?

* * * *

Devron and Karl realize they were in a rescue operation. They had found a live person, underwater, hidden somewhere beneath them in the rock. Momentarily, they wondered, "How could that person be alive down there? What do we do next?"

Neither of them is trained to deal with a rescue situation of any type. Questions flashed in their minds in the moment. What is the next step? How do we get him out? How long do we have before he is totally underwater? We can hear him, but neither of us knows exactly where he is. He is some place in the rocks. But where?

They were nervous, incredulous, and anxious. They had made contact with the proverbial "needle in the haystack".

Karl's first rational thought was that the person (he didn't even know my name) was probably very lonely and afraid. How do we keep in contact with him so that he knows he is no longer alone?

Going down the hole to perform a rescue was not possible. The next thing that came to mind was to get a rope. Devron took the role to go back to the shore to find-a rope. That left Karl to stay with the victim (who they learn is "Dean" by asking him his name) to keep verbal contact.

"I could feel his pain as he was talking with me," Karl, a very spiritual man recalled. "The weakness of his voice and the plaintive cries for *don't leave me* really hit me emotionally. I focused on staying connected to him; to transfer my strength to help with his desperate, weakened state."

Karl and I connected on some spiritual level. I knew in my heart that Karl was my lifeline. I needed his reassurance. Karl was projecting strength and optimism.

After Devron left, Karl continued to yell encouragement down the hole. "You are strong. Stay brave. You are a warrior. We are going to get a rope and pull you out of there. Stay with me."

I would respond whenever I could. Sometimes, the message was a simple affirmation, "I hear you". At other times, I tried to convey the desperation of my situation, cold, out of energy, beaten up by the rocks. "We need to hurry. I don't know how much longer I can hold on." Karl felt the building anxiety in my voice, and was feeling anxious himself. Would his and Devron's efforts be enough, soon enough? He could do nothing more than be there for me.

Summoning all of his voice, he kept encouraging me, telling me to stay strong. "We are going to get you out."

* * * *

As Rose and Stephen sat on the beach wondering what was going on with Karl and Devron, they had no hope of seeing me again. Rose thought of the picture Stephen had taken not too long before, realizing it would be the last picture of the two of us together. Even that was taken from her when she realized the picture was gone with her phone. She cried to herself, "We don't even have a final picture together."

Stephen alternated between pacing the beach and hugging Rose. He was a bundle of nervous energy, unable to do anything but keep moving.

Rose thought of the dragonflies encountered on our hike. My mom was nicknamed "libelula" (dragonfly) by her Romanian uncle years earlier. She got this name because she never sat still for long. Ever since she passed, when we see dragonflies, we know she is with us and all is well. Rose pondered, "How could this have happened? There were dragonflies all along the walk out to the tide pools."

All-of-a-sudden, there was movement coming back from the tide pools. The two of them stood up.

Devron ran back, giving them a two-thumbs up signal with a big smile. He announced, "We found him, he is alive. He is in the rocks and we are talking to him."

Stephen threw up three times on the beach that day. This was the first.

"That's not possible," was Rose's initial reaction. She almost fainted at the news, feeling her knees begin to buckle. Stephen help steady her.

"Oh no, poor Dean! He's trapped," ran through Rose's mind. "He's been trapped and alone all this time. He must be so frightened." The realization hit her hard that the two of them had walked away from me earlier because they thought I was dead. Now she was overcome with guilt that they had left me to die alone.

Rose had a new focus. "I couldn't go to the tidal pools to help because of my fear. I just stood looking toward the pools and began praying and sending every ounce of energy I could to Dean."

* * * *

After talking some time, Karl told me his name. Waiting for Devron to return, Karl and I communicated back-and-forth through the hole. He told me I was strong. He made sure I knew I had someone caring for me.

I longed to hear his voice in the moments when the water filled the hole, making communication impossible. When I could not hear him, I called out desperately, "Are you still there?", hoping that he had not left me. Sometimes I would hear him say something, but I could not understand it. I yelled out (as best I could) that I did not hear him. He would patiently repeat. It was hit-and-miss on trying to stay connected. But he did so for all the intervening minutes. It felt like a long time. He was my lifeline, even if there was no clear way out.

He also told me that his buddy, Devron, had gone to look for a rope. Now I knew there were two rescuers.

"You are being so strong."

"Hang in there, we are going to get you out."

"You are a warrior. You are brave. Hang on. Help is coming."

I tried my hardest to respond in kind, but with my diminished lung capacity it was not easy. I don't think I was ever afraid he was going to leave. Hearing his voice was reassuring. I wondered if I was going to be able to hang on much longer. Time was the enemy.

Chapter 5: The Rescue

"Men are alike in their promises. It is only in their deeds that they differ. The difference in their deeds is simple: People of character do what is right regardless of the situation". Moliere

Back at the beach, the next stroke of good luck was about to happen. What we characterize as miracle #2. Soon after Devron told Rose and Stephen the news that I was alive, another vehicle pulled up.

Ben Torkelson arrived in his Jeep with red and white strobe lights. Ben had taken the day off to show his brother, Drew, and his girlfriend, Jenna, the tide pools. He stopped to fill up with gas along the way. While at the gas station, he got a call from Jason (another Rescue St. Croix volunteer) that a 911 call said someone had been washed out to sea at the tide pools. Ben left the gas station almost immediately, now with a greater sense of urgency.

Since he was already planning on going there, he was only 10 minutes away from the road to the tide pools when he received the call, not 45 minutes away if he had still been home. He told Drew and Jenna that their day had changed. He asked Drew to text Jason to give him a status update: "I have reached the top of the hill leading to the beach and am heading down. As you know, during that trip down, I won't have cell service."

During the 30-minute drive on the very rugged road to the pools, he prepared Drew and Jenna for what was to come. Ben was a chaplain in the Marines and he knew this could be a potentially shocking and sad scene. "We are going to come across the family down there who are going to be dealing with a death, since the call said this was a body recovery mission." He was mentally preparing to put his chaplain's hat on to try to provide whatever support he could.

Ben is a stocky, no-nonsense, jack-of-all trades who exudes preparation and service. He strikes me as the kind of person in the neighborhood who would be good at fixing just about anything. In all the times I reached out to him for information or confirmation of facts, he got back to me quickly. I could count on him, just like I did on November 22.

He served in the Marines for five years and as a civilian working with the Army for a few years after that, including time in Iraq. Ben, as one of four Rescue St. Croix volunteers for the whole island supports EMTs, firefighters, police, and respond to 911 calls. Ben is a PADI licensed Master Scuba Diver. He and his wife, Stephanie, along with their three children moved to St. Croix in March 2021 "looking for something different".

He told me this incredible story that was one of the biggest keys to my rescue (emphasis mine):

"I was packing my Jeep because I have done rescues at the pools before. I packed up a shovel and threw it in the jeep. I brought my trauma bag because I tend to always have that with me. I grabbed my life vest and my oxygen tank and placed them in the trunk. I also decided to grab my rescue rope. I have **not carried my rescue rope in my Jeep for over a year** because I never have needed it. It had been sitting in my closet."

Upon arrival, Ben walked towards people on the beach. He was pointed toward two people, Rose and Stephen. Rose was on the phone with the Coast Guard 911 Command Center. When the Command Center heard a rescuer had arrived, they asked to have him get on the phone. The Command Center had very little information at this time, other than a drowning victim and a general location. They hoped Ben could fill in details like the GPS coordinates and the on-scene situation so they could relay information to other potential rescuers.

He learned that the Coast Guard cutter off the coast of the tide pools could not come in to assist in the body recovery. The wind and waves were too rough for the size of boat. They were there to support however they could, mainly with communications.

Having just arrived and with no information about the situation, he told them he needed to assess the situation, the currents, and figure out where everyone ought to start looking for the body.

That was when a civilian (who he learned is Devron) ran over and said, "We are talking to him, he is alive". Ben asked Devron to describe the situation he just came from. All that Devron could say in his excitement was, "we are talking to him through the rocks. We need a rope to pull him out."

Ben understood this new information made an immediate difference. The mission had changed from a recovery to a rescue. He relayed the new information he had to the Coast Guard Command Center, hung up the phone, and raced back to his Jeep. Now all of the equipment he had put in his Jeep had a purpose. Putting on his life vest and rock-climbing shoes, he grabbed his medical trauma bag. Last, but not least, he looked at the rescue rope he put in his Jeep at the last minute and pulled it out, knowing it was going to be very important. He and Devron ran down the beach, scaled over the rocks, and moved quickly to the spot where Karl was.

Devron and Ben arrived at the rocks, out of breath from the exertion and excitement. Karl was in a dangerous position, partially submerged in the water and yelling down the hole to me. Ben and Karl did a quick introduction and Karl filled Ben in on what he knew and what had happened. At first, Ben couldn't comprehend what Karl meant when he said, "He is in the rock". Ben was confused by what this meant, so Karl jumped down closer to the hole to show the spot where he believed I went down and how he had been communicating with me.

While there, Karl yelled to me, "Rescue is here and we are going to get you out."

Ben was still trying to make sense of all that had happened in the last few minutes. His mission, a recovery of a dead body, had turned into a rescue of a person who was trapped, but alive. "I have a lot of training, but this is not a scenario I have ever encountered," he thought to himself. Trying to gather his thoughts, he asked for my name a few times. Ben told the other two, "I wanted to hear him because I was talking to a rock and I had to hear a voice."

"I don't know how much longer I can hold on. I am extremely cold and it is hard to breath. Please hurry," I responded. Ben understood a sense of urgency was important.

While this was a unique rescue scenario for Ben, he was still able to rely on his training and to respond to a challenging situation. "I recognized that the three of us (he, Karl, and Devron) had never met before this minute. Now a life was on the line, and our ability to find a solution and work as a team was the key to all of us surviving. We had to improvise on the spot. Because I was the expert of the three, I needed to be the one calling the shots."

The first solution that came to his mind, send someone down the hole, was not feasible. The swirling water, sharp rocks, and their lack of underwater gear made it much too dangerous. They agreed to try tossing the rope down the hole and hope it who make it to where I was standing. From Ben's vantage point, the hole looked like it went down and then hooked to the right. But obscured in the whitewater could be many other twists and corners for the rope to get stuck on. They would have to throw the rope and hope it reached its intended target.

"I was concerned that Dean was in distress and in that teetering spot of fighting for life but growing much less strong," Ben said. "He'd come this far; I did not want him to give up this close to a potential rescue." He asked Karl to keep talking to me and let me know they were still with me.

The team of three were hit by waves, driven by the trade winds while standing on top of the volcanic rock. Devron, higher on the rock wall looking out to sea, called out when a wave was coming, as a warning. Ben reflected on his rescue training which was clear in its instructions: "don't turn your back to the ocean." But the nature of where they were and what they had to do put them in that position. "In my mind, I did not like turning my back to the ocean, but the rescue required it."

"As the waves keep coming in, the hole filled with water. Then the hole is all white water and I could not see it anymore," is how Ben described the scene. "All of a sudden, it was as if someone flushed a toilet. Water immediately sucked down and the hole empties part of the way. The hole is visible again. This occurs over-and-over as the waves come in and then rush back out to the ocean."

We later were able to measure the size of the hole. It is about 2.5 feet by 1.5 feet, which is slightly larger than the height and width of a carryon bag you may take on an airplane.

With the waves crashing on them, and the hole filling and emptying of water, Ben knew he had to find the right moment to throw the rope down the hole. But finding that right moment was a challenge.

His training and the rope were on swift water rescue. Those ropes are thrown out into a river where the rescuer can see the person and the water is moving horizontally. In this case, he was dropping a rope vertically down a hole to a person he could not see. He had to hope it went in the right direction without getting caught on the rocks.

Ben relayed to Karl, "Tell Dean we are going to send a rope to him."

"I wanted to estimate the amount of rope I let out so I could estimate how far away Dean was from us," Ben was thinking. "I believe I started letting out 25 feet. I was trying to remember how long the rope is, because as I let it out, it would tell me how far away Dean was. In the confusion and stress of the situation, it was hard to think entirely clearly. I could not remember the length of the rope."

Ben tried to time throwing the rope down with the rhythm of the waves. He allowed a couple waves to come and go as he held the rope, trying to gauge the frequency. He would use the suction of the water draining down the hole to try to get the rope to float to me.

"90% of the time, it is not going to work" was his thinking. The odds were stacked against him because he had to time the toss just right with the suction. Then the resulting water flow somehow had to take the rope into Dean's direction. The rope would have to avoid many rocks and twists that could block its path.

He told Karl again, "Tell him to look for a rope". Karl relayed back my reply, "A rope? How am I supposed to find a rope in here?"

"Tell Dean there is a basket attached to it that will make it float. Feel for it."

Ben let out more rope and all of a sudden, a wave grabbed it and sucked it down the hole. It flushed again and then the rope went tight. Ben tried to assess how much rope had gone in and hope it steered itself in the right direction after it went in the hole.

The three of them held their breath waiting to hear.

* * * *

Down in the hole, I had no idea what was going on above me. I communicated with Karl's disembodied voice yelling to me. That was my lifeline to the world. Having endured 40 minutes of silence prior to my connection with the voice I came to learn was Karl, I desperately wanted to stay connected.

With my diminishing strength, I did my best to yell back to him. My breathing was so shallow from all of the salt water I had consumed that speaking more than a couple words was barely possible. All of my attention and strength shifted to staying in connection with the voice. "Hurry, it is dangerous down here." He encouraged me and updated me what was going on with them. He told me they had a rope and were going to throw it to me.

The statement about a rope was totally confusing to me. Somehow, they want me to find a rope they intend to throw down to me. I am in the pitch-black dark hole. I cannot see a thing. Water is swirling all around me. I am weak and tired. I don't even know the direction the rope will come from.

Karl continued talking to me the whole time, as we alternated speaking between the waves crashing in on me. With my severely degraded health and lack of oxygen from taking in so much salt water, I was having trouble thinking.

I questioned him, "You want me to catch a rope? How am I supposed to get this rope?" It seemed too improbable. Catch a rope, of unknown size, from an unknown direction, coming sometime soon. And then hold onto the rope.

Since I could not see to grab the rope, I had to do something different. I simply stretched both of my arms straight out in front of me, palms up, and waited.

That is when the next miracle occurred.

I suddenly felt the rope, floating on the water, rubbing against my outstretched forearms. The rope had doubled back against itself a few times in its way to me. I grabbed as much as I could and held on.

I yelled back to Karl, "I've got the rope".

Karl talked me through their plan and the process that Ben relayed to him. I was not very coherent, so Karl had to repeat himself. I had been underwater, in this cave that I thought was my grave, for at least an hour. I had no idea how far they were going to drag me to get me out. I knew that I could only last a very few feet underwater holding my breath. My biggest fear now was drowning as they dragged me out by the rope. How horrible would it be to drown during the rescue after being found?

* * * *

After Ben had sent the rope down the hole, he waited. "The rope had beaten the long odds I had set in my mind just to go down the hole," he thought. He had originally felt 90% sure this was not going to work. At least the rope was below the surface, down there somewhere. But where?

He tugged on the rope and felt it stuck. Over the next few moments, he waited and wondered. Had the rope caught on a rock? Was it jammed against a corner? Did it even reach Dean? Was this rope going to work in this circumstance?

"There was no way to steer it, so where was the rope?" he told me later. "Somehow, the waves and the water had to bring the rope to

Dean. I was now as much in the dark as Dean was. I waited those long seconds hoping to hear something. What was I going to do if the rope did not reach him?"

Ben was broken out of his musing by the sound of Karl's triumphant voice, "Dean has the rope!"

He relayed to Karl, "Tell him I am going to start tugging on the rope. Ask him if he can feel me tugging on it". From his perspective, the rope had gotten tight. It did not move. Was it possible that the rope was hung up on a rock?

Karl yelled out to me and waited for a response. I yelled back, "I can feel someone tugging on the rope." By some miracle, the rope had made it to me, unobstructed.

Time slowed down. I did not move from the ledge I was standing on. I was still afraid of the abyss around me. I assumed it was a greater ocean depth. Having spent a harrowing time afraid to check out the area I was trapped in, I was now being instructed to "jump in". My brain was not ready to do that.

Because I had ahold of multiple strands of the rope, I let go of part of it. I figured I would hold onto the very end.

Ben recalled, "As I would tug the rope, there would be some resistance, and then it would go slack. Every time that happened, I got worried that we lost Dean. I asked Karl to check with Dean, 'do you still have the rope?'.

I told them I still had it. I did not have enough strength to explain I was letting go of part of it.

Eventually, I reached the end of the rope and it was time to trust. It had been what felt like an eternity since the rope first came to me. While I knew the rope was my lifeline, I was so scared for a number of reasons. The ledge, although it was in a dark cave with water swirling around it, was more of a known then leaving it and hoping the rope would lead me out of the cavern. My breathing was so labored that I did not think I could hold it long enough to survive. I felt no strength in my body. Could I hold the rope? I was frozen in indecision.

Karl continued to encourage me, "We've got you. Let us pull you up."

I was apprehensive to take that leap of faith even though it was the only way out. In my confused state of mind, I could not reason. Once I committed to getting off my ledge, that was it. My one chance. None of us knew how far they would drag me. We did not know the path out. We had to trust the rope to do that.

I now had the end of the rope, holding onto the basket it came in with both hands. I did not jump immediately. Was it fear? Was I trying to get myself mentally prepared? I do not know.

Eventually, I jumped into the water holding the rope.

Up on the rocks, Ben, Karl, and Devron waited anxiously. Ben said to the other two, "He is going to have to rescue himself. We can't go get him. Keep encouraging him to jump."

Ben pulled the rope hard and felt it go slack. He called out to Karl. Karl said, "He's not talking. I don't have him anymore." Ben started reeling in the rope, hand over hand, winding it back up. What had happened?

"As I pulled it, the rope got tight again and I started pulling harder," Ben recalled. "All of a sudden, I saw a finger, then the yellow rope wrapped around a hand, and an arm coming up out of the hole. Karl grabbed for the arm, but the combination of water and blood made it slippery. I grabbed the hand I saw. Karl jumped down into the pool and grabbed the other arm. It was all so sudden. Instinctual. We yanked Dean up. I fell backwards onto my butt, bear hugging him on top of me onto the rocks. We had him out."

* * * *

I remember emerging from the hole into the light of day. This was my first time in an hour breathing the fresh air, seeing the sun, and feeling the ocean breeze. I was in so much shock that I could not process everything. I will forever remember seeing the person who I learned was Devron turning to the beach and signaling with both thumbs up, indicating that I was rescued.

The best we can guess is that the path out of the hole was a left bend out towards the sea (away from the rescuers), then a sharp turn to the right, and then up vertically through the hole. Turns out I would never have been able to self-rescue. I would have had to navigate those turns in the dark. The last part of the journey was a vertical shot against the current of the water. I did not have the strength to pull off that feat.

I've been asked numerous times if I tied the rope around my body. That would have been the logical thing to do, but I did not have any brain capacity working for me by then. I simply held on to the rope with both hands. How I had the physical strength to hold onto the rope as they pulled me up and out, against the water flow, I will never know. I don't even know if I was conscious that this was happening. From their perspective, I was totally limp when they pulled me out of the hole.

Ben said to me later, "you looked like chewed up hamburger". But I am alive. Ben said he grabbed me by my swim trunks and gave me a major wedgie to make sure I was out of the hole.

This was a major victory, but there was still work to be done. Now that I was out, the team needed to get me away from the hole to a slightly safer part of the rocks. They still needed to assess my condition, but they could tell I was in bad shape. They had to balance being careful and getting me to a safer spot on the rocks quickly.

Chapter 6: Reflections on Survival

"When we approach our own suffering with curiosity, asking it what may have to teach us, it takes on new meaning" Gladys McGarey "The Well-Lived Life"

Why did I survive?

It is very humbling to know that I beat the odds, surviving in the cavern all that time and then the miracle of the rescue. We all know people who go through tragedies and don't survive. The victims of hurricanes, fires, and other natural disasters who did not get saved. Those who are diagnosed with cancer or other-life-ending diseases do not have the chance to do more with their lives. Victims of random acts of violence did not have their "guardian angel watching over them". They were all "in the wrong place at the wrong time", similar to me. Why did I survive and they did not?

In his book, *The Eye Test*, author Chris Jones writes about the uncertainty of life:

"It was hard . . . to think that something as sacred as life could depend on such randomness, on luck, on the uncontrollable and the unknowable, on dumb circumstance. Survivors often suffer through the same agonizing calculus. The sum, more often than not, is guilt. Why not them? Why me? Nobody knows why. Maybe none of us is meant to know."

While I do not feel guilty about what happened to me, I do wonder about the randomness of it all. I am not better, no more valuable, no more deserving than anyone else to live. Why did I live? It is unknowable. But I do think about it when I read passages like the one above.

Later in the same book, Jones wrote about Kenneth Feinberg, special master of the 9/11 Victim Compensation Fund. Feinberg was tasked with deciding how much money each person and family impacted by 9/11 would be compensated. He had to answer questions like, "how much is a life worth?". His approach for a long time was very logical, very mathematical, very equitable. He was convinced he was right. Until he realized he wasn't right, couldn't be right, anymore. Jones writes:

"That's what has changed the most about Kenneth Feinberg: He was once a man of certainty, a man of laws who saw the world in black-and-white . . .Now he is filled with doubt. He understands better than most of us that life is not linear. We can't know what the future will bring. Today represents the end of our understanding, the outer limits of the world of fact."

I can relate to that. Feinberg had a hard decision to make. Once he had it figured out, he thought all was well. Then his plan met reality, the uncertainty that fills our lives. That is why he was filled with doubt.

I cannot judge why I lived, so I should not. I was standing in the water as close to shore as possible facing the ocean, nothing bad could happen. Then something bad happened. Our certainty is our weakness.

We all try to come up with the answer as to why something happened. Disorder is not comfortable. We fill in a story's gaps to explain why someone has something bad happen to them. For example, in ancient times, anyone with a disability was looked upon as someone who had done something wrong in God's eyes or was paying the price for transgressions of family members. Someone with leprosy was believed to be ill as the punishment for their sins. In the 1500 and 1600s, if a woman displayed the symptoms of epilepsy, they were branded "witches".

We all search for an explanation. A neat and tidy answer. Why did Dean survive? It was God's will. Or, Dean was in good shape, that is what saved him.

I remember my mindset, soon after the event, when I heard those comments. When others wanted to give God the credit, I viewed it as downplaying my role and the rescuers' roles in saving me.

When others said I was particularly brave, I wanted to downplay my role in being saved. I was scared in the hole, not heroic. I knew the situation was hopeless. I had doubts. I am not that strong. While I was not claustrophobic that was probably because I was so focused on drowning that I did not think about it. I was not heroic. I did not want people to say I was brave.

Over time, I began to understand that all of us were simply trying to put some order into a very tough, unknowable situation. Rather than downplay each person's reaction, I came to accept them. If it helps the other person feel more comfortable having a partial answer, why not support it? After all, we can never know the whole truth.

My survival was not easily explainable. We won't know the answer until we meet God. While still on earth, you may have your own answer to that question, "why did Dean survive?"

Chapter 7: On the Rocks

"We cannot accomplish all that we need to do without working together" - Bill Richardson

I was pulled from the hole at about 1:30 p.m., nearly two hours after Rose, Stephen, and I had first arrived at the beach. Those two hours had been filled with shocking and difficult events. But the day was far from over. Now a new phase began.

On the one hand, I feel a sense of relief. I am out of the water. On the rocks. I am in the care of others. But I am not feeling physically great.

The top of the wall is littered with rocks, large and small. It's like a debris field from a flood. The rocks I lay on are very sharp. There is no flat ground to lay on, so wherever my body rests, I feel different rocks uncomfortably prodding my body.

Having been submerged in water for an hour, my body temperature is approaching hypothermia. I was exposed to the breeze. Waves crash on top of us, continuously. Even though the air temperature is 85 degrees, I am very cold because my internal temperature dropped so low while under the rocks.

We are all positioned right above the hole I was just rescued from. If any of the rescuers slipped or fell, they were in danger of being sucked down the hole. We needed to get somewhere else.

"I was worried that we might lose our grip because of the water and the blood, dropping Dean back into the hole," Ben noted. He recognized the need to get up on the rock further away from the water. However, he had not assessed my health yet. Rescuers are taught to assess first, move only if necessary, in order to avoid exacerbating the injuries. Ben had to make an immediate decision.

"I needed to prioritize life over limb," Ben thought. "It is possible Dean has a spinal injury, but we needed to move to a safer spot." We all moved about six feet higher on the rocks and away from the hole.

Ben assessed my health situation.

There was blood all over Ben and me. Ben thought to himself "does he have a head injury? There has to be broken bones or something more that has happened to cause all of the blood." In this new, safer spot, he did a trauma assessment of my abdomen, neck, and head wound that was bleeding. He did not see anything major, a surprise given the situation and the blood.

Karl allowed me to lean against him as he held my head steady. He kept talking to me. I told him I was having trouble breathing. Hearing this, Ben tried to check my blood oxygen level using the SPO2 monitor. Unfortunately, the monitor does not work well with cold skin. The first reading he got was a blood oxygen level of 66. He knew that was a fatal level (99 is normal). Not being a medical professional, he did not know what to make of such a low level. The fact that I was responsive made him feel the reading might be inaccurate. Ben brought out his oxygen tank and started to administer oxygen.

Now that I was out of the hole, my mind focused on all of the discomfort I was in. When I was in the hole, I did not think about my body. With all of the cuts and bruises I had suffered from being repeatedly slammed into the rock walls now exposed to the air, I hurt all over. I moaned from the pain and the discomfort in a very weak voice, "I am so cold". My body was telling me how cold it was. The wind was cold on my suddenly exposed body. Every wave that crashed onto the rocks sent a spray of cold water, drenching all of us. It was agony for me. I was so weakened; I could not move on my own.

Ben wondered how we were going to me off those rocks and back onto the shore. No other responders were around yet to help. There was only the three of them. The bad condition I was in and the increasingly strong waves was making the extraction much tougher.

* * * *

After receiving the original 911 call, three more groups of responders began converging on road to the tide pools. One vehicle held the ambulance driver and EMTs. Another had firefighters and a third had another Rescue St. Croix volunteer. They all met at the

Carambola Resort parking lot. Malik Garvey, on his first day as an ambulance driver, quickly discerned the ambulance could not make it down the steep, bumpy road to the tide pools. The Rescue St. Croix volunteer, Jason Henry, took charge. He told everyone to get into his vehicle and come together. That meant each of them made a hurried decision on what rescue/medical equipment to bring before jumping into Jason's Jeep.

The "road" to the beach is only a couple miles long, but it is not a road. It is a path carved into the jungle by water moving downward after a rainstorm. Most of the time, it is a dry, very steep, rutted, and hard-to-navigate path straight down the side of the hill. It took at least 30 minutes to get from the top to the beach, approximately two miles.

It was around 1:40 p.m. when they reached the beach. Soon thereafter, they heard for the first time that I was found alive. As Malik said, "Hearing the news that the victim was alive, the mission changed from a body recovery to a rescue. Our mood changed quickly."

Three of them, Jason (who knew Ben very well from having worked with him on numerous incidents), Malik, and Shumba sprang into action. Without hesitation, the three of them ran to join the group on the rocks. The rest of the crew stayed behind.

After the three new rescuers navigated the 300 yards to the pools, they spotted Ben and asked "What do you need?" Ben told them he needed oxygen to aid my breathing, and towels to dry me off. The new group had neither with them. They had left oxygen behind in the parking lot when they had to consolidate into one vehicle and bring limited supplies. No one had towels, but Malik and Shumba gave their shirts to try to cover some of my body from the cold water and wind.

Devron and Malik reversed course, taking off back to the beach to see if they could get towels.

"I did not know any of the other guys, but having Jason there was a big comfort," Ben noted. "We are two of the four Rescue St. Croix volunteers on the island. We had worked together a lot. We each knew the other's capabilities. His arrival provided a boost of hope."

Jason and Ben immediately split up duties. Jason took over as the Incident Commander (IC), in charge of figuring out the rescue. He got on his phone with the Coast Guard boat and with the 911 Center in San Juan, confirming we had a rescue. Ben had the role of operations/EMT lead. His job was to get me medically stable with the little equipment he had, keep me warm, and make sure I did not go into shock.

Karl remained at his "post", on the rocks, holding my head and upper torso. He used every ounce of his strength to talk to me, to comfort me, and to tell me to be strong. Devron, Malik, and Shumba formed a relay team to bring dry towels and clothes. They went to the beach and got whatever they could from the assortment of people who were there. Upon return, the three of them alternated watching for the waves, calling out when a big one was going to crash, and helping cover my body against the ravages of the harsh waves. Ben administered oxygen from the one tank he had brought with him.

Once everyone had a role, Jason and Ben assessed the options for getting off the rocks. They knew in my severely weakened condition that I was not going to walk out of there. I could not even sit up. They debated whether they could carry me out. The trip back to shore was hard, but doable for a healthy person only responsible for themselves. Trying to carry out a severely injured man, whose condition they did not fully know, across slippery rocks with waves pounding them, without a stretcher, was not viable.

They made a decision to request deployment of a Coast Guard rescue helicopter. Unfortunately, the helicopter was '45 minutes out' (it ended up being much longer than that), because it had to come from San Juan, Puerto Rico. With the extraction decision made, Jason called the Command Center in San Juan at 1:46 p.m., relayed the situation (it is no longer a body recovery, it is a rescue operation), and requested a helicopter be deployed. This was about 90 minutes since I first went down the hole.

Jason and Ben pondered a plan B if the helicopter did not get deployed or if they could not wait for the helicopter to arrive. Could I last another hour or two on those rocks while we waited for the helicopter?

One option was quickly rendered impractical. Ben walked down the rocks to check out the terrain. In his mind, the rocks got sharper and more jagged, like razor blades, as he walked along the rock wall. If someone were to slip on those rocks, there was a high risk of serious injury. Having to carry me out while walking on those slippery, sharp rocks was deemed a high-risk situation.

The next idea was to float me out on a backboard with life jackets to provide floatation out of the tidepools. The problem with that idea was it put all of us at risk if a big wave came in and flipped us over. After the pools (but before the beach) there is a stretch of open water where the waves slam into the rocks. Normally, an individual walks over those rocks, remaining above the waves, to get to shore. That was not happening by 1:45 that day.

They considered tying one end of a rope to a back board and throwing the other end to the people on the beach. They could reel me in while someone with a life jacket in the water was keeping the board I was on afloat. They decided that plan was too risky because of the waves.

As this planning was going on, I lay there moaning from the pain and from feeling so cold. The spray from the waves sent shivers all over my very cold body. Whatever shirts and towels that had been provided were soaked and did not provide much comfort. The rescuers were all doing their best, but the lack of resources and the worsening weather was making the situation tougher. A rain squall was starting to move into the area.

Karl remained with me. Ben was at my left side by my head, asking how I was doing and trying to assess my health. He administered oxygen. He told me "You are MY patient and I am doing everything I can for you."

Each of the rescuers took turns talking to me, doing everything to keep my eyes open and not to go into shock. I was not very coherent. But it did lead to a couple funny stories.

Jason asked me, "Would you like a cup of hot coffee right now?" I responded, in a not so nice way, that I don't drink coffee. He tried to get me to agree to go with him and he would drink tea and I would drink coffee. He tried again, "Would you like some warm chicken soup?" I turned that down, too.

They asked me where I was from. I told them, "Dayton, Ohio". For some reason, I decided it was important to tell them that Dayton was the "home of the Wright Brothers." I guess I was giving a small history lesson. They chuckled when I told them that bit of history.

Ben decided that he had to cut my shorts off me to make sure there was no other injuries or bleeding. Anyhow, the shorts were soaked and were only making me colder. I got agitated at the suggestion that he was going to ruin my shorts. Perhaps it was because this was the first time that I had ever worn those shorts and did not want to lose them. But he cut them off me. I was buck naked on the rocks, freezing cold.

All of us on the rocks were getting regularly pummeled by waves. One person watched out for waves and warned the team a wave was coming. When they got the verbal notification, everyone leaned over me, sacrificing their bodies by covering me to keep the waves from hitting me as much as they could. It was cold, hard work. A few times, the amount of water coming over the rock wall was enough to lift me into the air momentarily. They did their best to hold me from floating away.

I heard Jason communicating with the Coast Guard boat and with the Coast Guard Command Center to give them updates. Unfortunately, his phone was running out of power. He told us all that the helicopter would be here in an hour.

Chapter 8: Waiting and Wondering

"Life does not ask us what we want. It presents us with options."
Thomas Sowell

For Rose and Steve on the beach, this was a time of confusion, hope, and anxiety. They knew I was alive. But they had no idea of my condition. They were encouraged seeing so many rescuers. Their view out to the rocks where I lay was limited due to the height of the rocks and the curvature of the shoreline. They had no detailed knowledge of what was happening.

"I alternatively stood and sat on the beach praying constantly," Rose remembers. "Frankly, I was afraid to hope. I wouldn't or couldn't let my brain think the best or the worst. I just prayed constantly. Mostly, I did the rosary over and over with please Lord, please have mercy, Lord. Lord please."

Stephen moved between consoling his mom, pacing on the beach, and talking with others. John, Amie, and the families that were originally brought to the Tide Pools by Karl and Devron stayed with them.

Suddenly, Amie said that she could see the three (Ben, Devron, and Karl) had me out of the hole. She saw Devron stand up and signal with two thumbs up. John zoomed in picture of the scene on the rocks on his camera. It showed someone sitting up, but it was so far away, they could not tell if it was me or not. It was too blurry to tell.

Confirmation came quickly. Devron ran and told them that I was out of the hole. Stephen and Rose started crying and hugging each other.

"I have never shaken and cried that much in my life," Stephen said. "Hearing my dad was out of the hole was the second time I threw up that day. Mom and I were holding each other and crying. Convulsing, shaken with a rush of emotion and relief. He was alive."

Devron asked Stephen if he would like a picture so he could see me. Stephen noted, "Devron took pictures of dad on the rocks, even though he was not supposed to, using my phone. He brought my phone back to me and I looked at the pictures. I did not tell mom I had them because dad did not look good at all."

On the beach, Rose and Stephen felt hopeless to do any specific action, but now had hope since they knew I was alive. They didn't know what condition I was in and whether I was getting better or getting worse. Rose offered to go out to the rocks and hold me to warm me. The rescuers told her that was not going to happen because it was dangerous enough for them with the wind and the waves.

While the two of them had each other to lean on, they were each trying to come to grips with the last hour. Stephen continued to look out for Rose. Rose remembered him saying, "Mom, today is going to be the worst and best day of our life."

Rose searched for ways to be more positive. "I looked down at my feet. There was a small piece of driftwood. Dean always liked driftwood. I picked it up and held on to it for him. He could decide if we would take it home. But it felt like a connection between the two of us. That is what I felt we both needed at that moment."

Stephen was going through numerous thoughts and emotions. "I thought a few times, what if I had got sucked down the hole with my dad? Would we have tried to save each other? Would there be enough oxygen for the two of us? Would I have even gone to the same place? What would my mom do if we were both gone? I know it was not useful, but it came into my mind a few times."

"I realized how tense the situation was. I knew how I felt almost getting sucked down the hole to my death. What was it like for my dad?"

Two paramedics (who had come in the group of people crammed into Jason's vehicle) remained on the beach in the general vicinity. They gave Rose and Stephen whatever information was relayed by Jason from the rocks. They knew my vital numbers were terrible. They also knew I was conscious, responsive, and talking. The paramedics were trusting the reports, not the numbers, "if he is talking, he is not as bad as the numbers would indicate. It is a good sign we are not out there on the rock; if we were called out there, it would mean he is in very bad shape".

Reaching for any news that sounded positive, Rose and Stephen clung to those comments.

On one of his trips back to shore to get warm items for me, rescuer Malik told them a call had been made for a helicopter to get me off the rocks.

"I am accustomed to what you see on tv. I thought it would take a couple minutes for the helicopter to arrive. It took a lot longer than that," Stephen recalled. "The waiting was torture. I had so little information."

When Devron and Malik came back to shore looking for towels, shirts, blankets, anything to keep me warm, things felt a little more real to Rose The families on shore gave what they had. Everybody who was there quite literally gave the shirt off their backs. Running back-and-forth, Devron and Malik brought whatever they could onto the rocks.

John and Amie, whose 911 call started the whole chain of events, reluctantly had to leave to get to their cruise ship. Rose thanked them so much for all that they had done for us. Stephen made sure he had their phone number so that he could report back to them.

It was hard only having a verbal report on my condition. The minutes crawled by.

"What was going on? How were they going to get him to the shore? What was his condition? When was this going to end?" All those questions raced through Rose's mind. It was frustrating not knowing. But the uncertainty of the situation substituted for the dismay of the original thought that Dean was dead.

Chapter 9: US Coast Guard Comes to the Forefront

Semper Paratus ("Always Ready"). The US Coast Guard motto

About 105 miles from St. Croix in San Juan, Puerto Rico, the US Coast Guard Command Center was doing their daily duty receiving 911 calls. They had taken the earlier call that "someone had fallen into the water." At 1:46 p.m. Atlantic Time, a call from one of the rescuers, Jason, notified them of the change in situation. The Center learned I was alive and had been extracted. They had to gather whatever information they could to make a quick decision on what assets to deploy.

The US Coast Guard has been in existence since 1790. In the Caribbean area, they are focused on four main tasks: Search & Rescue, Drug Interdiction, Migrants, and maintaining integrity of ports in the Nation's Maritime Transportation System.

The Sector San Juan, Puerto Rico area of responsibility extends approximately 1.3 million square miles, a size greater than all of the land in the United States east of the Mississippi River. Coast Guard Air Station Borinquen is located at Rafael Hernandez Airport on the northwest tip of Puerto Rico, two hours west of San Juan.

The Coast Guard Air Station Borinquen ships and helicopters have three major duties: search and rescue, assisting with migrants looking to enter the US, and law enforcement, especially drug interdiction.

The Command Center did not have a lot of information about exactly where the rescue needed to take place and what the surrounding terrain looked like. They knew the Coast Guard cutter ship could not make it in to rescue me. Could a helicopter do so?

Their decision was complicated because helicopters are valuable and very limited resources. Every day, the Command Center has a number of calls come in for issues such as people overboard a boat, migrants trying to boat into US territory, or bad accident scenes. Do they risk sending a helicopter a long way away to possibly participate in a rescue of a badly injured 66-year-old man? Or do they keep the helicopter back in Air Station Borinquen in anticipation of other needs?

Luckily for us, they trusted the information from the rescue volunteers on the scene. The Command Center called the Air Station to alert the helicopter crew to get ready. A final decision would be made based on whatever additional information could be supplied by St. Croix and the readiness of the helicopter crew. Time was of the essence.

At 2:07 p.m., an alarm went off in the Air Station. The on-duty MH-60T Jayhawk helicopter crew had been going through their normal duties. The four of them were on a 24-hour shift that was to end at 4:00 p.m., but now they were getting ready for an extended working day.

The on-duty crew was Aircraft Commander William "Travis" Cox, Co-pilot William "Billy" Boardman, aviation maintenance technician Beau James, Jr., and Curren Hinote, aviation survival technician.

They knew on days like this one, when the trade winds were strong, waves can be much higher. The initial message relayed to them was that someone was "stuck on the rocks" in St. Croix. None of them had ever been to the tide pools, so they did not have a point of reference.

It took 23 minutes to gather gear, check the readiness of the helicopter, and collect the latest information. Their mission was a go. After takeoff, Beau went through rescue check #1. This is akin to checking to make sure everything is packed in your car before leaving on vacation.

This mission was the first time this group of four had ever worked together. The nature of the schedules for each of their roles means that the members of the crews vary all the time. Now, four individuals would transform into a team and execute a flight of at least one hour to arrive on the scene, perform a rescue of indeterminant time, and work together to deliver a rescued person and themselves to safety. It was a complicated mission, with no margin for error.

Each crew member has pre-defined set of responsibilities. The training and the professionalism of the US Coast Guard builds trust between four people who had not worked together before.

Beau relayed to the rest of the team that rescue check #1 had passed inspection. With clearance from the Command Center, they began their journey southeast across Puerto Rico towards St. Croix. They flew directly over Puerto Rico, across the Caribbean Sea, and over the mountains of St. Croix. It took about one hour flying time.

When the helicopter arrived on scene, the first challenge was to find the victim and the rescuers. From a vantage point a couple hundred feet up, it is not easy to spot a person. They did not have exact coordinates.

A 32-foot Coast Guard cutter boat was out on the ocean, having responded to the call for help. The crew of the cutter had quickly determined it was much too dangerous for them to bring the boat close to the rocks to attempt a rescue. They stayed out a hundred feet and served as a communication post for the rescuers and for the helicopter. The boat aided the helicopter by pointing in the direction of the rescue. Even with this help, the helicopter's first pass flew past us on the rocks, headed towards the larger group of people on the beach.

Beau, in the back of the helicopter, kept searching the area and told the cockpit that he saw a group of people on the rocks and felt that was where the rescue had occurred. Travis rerouted the helicopter a few hundred feet to check out Beau's intuition. It proved to be correct.

Now it was time for rescue check #2. Beau led this check, verbally calling out items as he verified them ("hoist hydraulics on, backup systems engaged", etc.). The final part of this check was to begin the rescue plan. They discerned this was not going to be an easy mission.

The first major assessment was how to get the rescue swimmer, Curren, down safely. They surveyed the area to see if they could land the helicopter somewhere nearby. The rocky terrain and cliffs on shore made landing impractical.

Not being able to land, they looked for a safe spot to drop Curren. The location of the rescue on the rocks was dangerously close to the cliff on shore. The wind was starting to pick up. The two choices for the drop were in the water or on the rocks. While Commander Cox flew the plane, the others assessed the situation, scanning the whole area, and checking for additional hazards.

Observing the waves slamming against the rocks, the team decided a water drop was not going to be safe. Putting Curren into the water, expecting him to swim to the rocks, and safely climb up the rocks looked too dangerous. They decided to use a cable to place Curren on the rocks.

With the drop decision made to lower Curren by cable, Travis circled again to get everything in the helicopter prepared. Curren put on his wet suit and harness. Beau got the hoist and its cable ready. The two of them tested that both the hoist and the harness were working properly. This activity took more time, as the helicopter made another pass, circling out to the ocean and around shore, back to the tide pool.

Once Beau gave the ready signal, pilot Travis maneuvered the helicopter into place and began lowering Curren down. Beau, in the back, directed the pilots up front in the cockpit over the radio how to lower Curren safely the last 20 feet to the ground. Beau was effectively flying the helicopter from the back and the pilots were following his commands.

* * * *

While all of this activity was going on, Rose and Stephen waited anxiously for the helicopter to complete its mission. On one of his trips back to the beach for more dry towels, Malik had told them the helicopter was going to be part of the rescue. They had no idea why we needed a helicopter and why it was going to take so long. The hardest part was not knowing the full story. Rose wondered "Why was it taking so long?" The feeling of numbness was gone, but it was only replaced by concern.

Once the helicopter arrived, it took longer than Stephen and Rose thought it should. They were thinking it would be like the movies where the hero swoops down, picks up the victim, and is off to safety, quickly. Stephen thought, "It's a five-minute operation in my mind. That turned out to be wrong." Much to their dismay, the helicopter made many circular passes over the area (we later learned it was 8 passes).

"Get him off the rock. Now! I was now concerned this helicopter rescue might not happen. I assumed they only had one or two shots to get dad off the rocks," Stephen remembers thinking. "The waves were getting worse. The chopper downdraft is making the wind stronger. I am thinking, 'What if they can't get dad off the rocks? He is now going to die on the rocks because they cannot get him off.' The anxiety and doubt were horrible." To top it off, rain clouds appeared on the ocean.

It had been more than two hours since I first went down the hole. Time continued to pass very slowly. Getting nearly no information about what was going on, all Rose could do was pray. She thought, "It was such a tense time; my insides were churning. I was exhausted."

Rose looked down by her feet and spotted a piece of coral. She thought, "It felt like it was presented to me, like the driftwood, a gift from the ocean. I picked it up and continued to hope."

Back on the rocks, the rescuers and I waited. The waves would come at irregular intervals and batter us with more cold water. The effort to keep me comfortable met more problems. Ben had instant hot packs, but none of them worked. He had a mylar blanket to wrap around me to retain heat. A wave ripped it in half. We moved again because the place on the rocks we were laying was getting pounded by waves.

Ben was doing all he could to keep me strong. He said to me, "You fought hard enough. It is not time to give up yet, but let us fight with you now. You have to stay awake."

As the oxygen tank ran out, Ben asked for more oxygen. He was frustrated that no one else brought more oxygen. My breathing was very labored, more like gasping for breath repeatedly.

It was as hard on the rescuers as it was on me. I knew they were trying to keep a very injured person alive and safe on a rock wall with strong winds and cold waves battering them. They were focused on me, but that does not mean they were not suffering, too.

Every time the helicopter came by, the downdraft from the propellers would sweep up water and small pieces of rocks. These would pummel us, adding to the difficulty and discomfort on the rocks. With most of the rescuers without shirts (given to me) and being soaked by the waves, it was particularly hard on them. But their focus was on the rescue. Every pass made me colder and wetter.

Jason received the radio message about the drop of the rescue swimmer. They watched as he was lowered safely onto the rocks about 30 feet east of us. He walked along the rock wall to get to us and told us his name was Curren.

The helicopter left the area again to give Curren time to assess the situation and to keep from splashing us all with the rotor wash. He was probably the youngest of the professionals there, but it was Curren's decision on how the rescue was to be made.

Jason and Ben briefed him: "We told him of Dean's condition - elevated blood pressure, dangerously low blood/oxygen level, and very cold." Since Curren also has paramedic training, he wanted to assess my condition. As he looked at me, he noticed that my eyes had a gray ring around them. He asked me, "Do you have cataracts?" I told him, "No."

Based on my condition and the look of the tide pools, Curren quickly rejected any idea of carrying me to the beach. The next option was to put me in a harness and have me hold on as they pulled me up to the helicopter. He could tell immediately that I was too weak for that option.

That left one option: lower a Stokes Basket (also known as a Stokes Litter) from the helicopter. With that decision made, Curren reached for his communication device with the helicopter only to find out the device was not functioning. He did not have direct communication to the helicopter, or a means to tell them what the plan would be.

****

After safely dropping Curren, the helicopter returned to a higher altitude to reduce the rotor winds for everyone on the rocks while Curren assessed the situation. After two more passes, they saw that Curren and the rescuers were still talking, which seemed excessive. When they did not hear by the time the third pass was beginning, they decided to get lower and tip the helicopter wings to get Curren's attention. At that pass, Curren gave a hand signal because he could not talk to them directly due to the device malfunction that he wanted a litter (Stokes Basket) drop.

With the signal to get the litter ready, the helicopter rose again, much to Rose and Stephen's dismay on the beach. What was going on? Had they run into unexpected trouble? The lack of information was hard to handle. Given their predisposition based on the movies, they thought the worst. All the two of them could do was hug each other.

Back in the helicopter, Beau assembled the Stokes Basket to get it ready for dropping down on the rocks. "The litter is not my favorite. I have to do a lot of rearranging of items in a cramped space to get to it," he said. "Then it needs to be assembled in a hot, confined space." It took three more "laps" and about five minutes to get everything ready for the litter's deployment.

All this time, the waves continued to pound us on the rocks. The oxygen tank was empty, so I was no longer getting that assistance. The towels and shirts covering me were soaking wet. Each pass of the helicopter brought more wind, more water being kicked up, and small rock pieces flying around. It was not a comfortable time for any of us. I had no idea what was going on. I was in pain, uncomfortable, and not very conscious. Everyone tried to keep me awake, and I was moaning a lot. Karl stayed with me, holding my head and upper back, motivating me.

Curren came over again to check on me and thought to himself, "this guy is not in great condition." He did not share that assessment with me, only saying, "You are in really good shape for what you had been through. You are a real warrior."

It had been nearly three and a half hours since I initially went down the hole. The rescuers and I had been up on the rocks for more than two hours, battling the waves and winds, striving to keep me from going in shock with their limited first aid equipment.

Once Beau had it ready, getting the Stokes Litter down to the rescuers was a tricky maneuver. At that spot on the rocks, they were about 30 feet from an angled cliff side. This made helicopter maneuvering very delicate. Travis angled the helicopter northwards into the wind to aid in hovering. Co-pilot Billy watched the tail very closely to ensure they did not get too close to the cliff.

The wind had picked up with the incoming rain storm and the currents were changing. It was a dangerous time. They had the helicopter about 100 feet in the air and began lowering the basket via a cable down to the rocks. Because a helicopter is not built to hover in one place, it took all four of them to make it work right.

After meeting them much later, Rose remarked that the helicopter crew looks like they came "directly from central casting for a movie". All of them are well-built, stand ramrod straight, and carry an air of competence.

The pilot, Aircraft Commander Travis Cox, is the most experienced and clearly the leader. Soft-spoken with a gravitas to his voice, he projects thoroughness and calmness (Rose later remarked, "his demeanor was like that of Tom Hanks in Apollo 13"). The way he looks you directly in the eye projected a sense of caring and empathy. He is a leader who you want to follow and you can count on to keep his wits in tough situations.

Lieutenant JG Billy Bordman, the co-pilot, is an earnest, serious second-in-command. Most important endeavors need someone who is mission focused and unconcerned with personal glory. Billy performs specific duties that are often out of the limelight, yet are critical to mission success such as being the main communication hub. Being a key link in a successful mission drives him. Rose, who loves to make movie references, compared Billy to the "loyal sidekick" in so many movies.

Beau James, Jr., aviation maintenance technician, appears to be a man of few words. His tasks (equipment maintenance, running the hoist, etc.) require tactile and physical strength. With his Clark Kent glasses, you sense there is more to him than meets the eye.

Curren Hinote has the qualities that you might imagine in a Formula One race driver: dashing, energetic, with a glint in his eye that says he does not fear danger. Like those race car drivers, as a "Rescue Swimmer" he descends into dangerous situations, but is well aware of the fine line between doing what is needed and being foolhardy. His desire to "be part of something bigger than himself" fits his role because he could not do what he does without the help of his crewmates.

* * * *

With Curren guiding the basket utilizing a trail line attached to it and Beau calling out maneuvers the basket made it down safely. Once Curren unhooked it, the helicopter pulled the cable back up and left the rescuers again.

A Stokes Basket or Litter is a metal/plastic wire frame that goes around a stretcher or backboard shaped to accommodate an adult in a face up position. It has a hook on the top that attaches to a cable that winches it up to a helicopter. If you have ever seen a movie with someone being hoisted up into a helicopter, the person was probably laying on a Stokes Litter.

With the litter safely down, the rescuers and Curren carried me over to it on the tarp I had been laying on. I was secured in by some straps along the frame of the litter. It was time for me to take a ride. Curren signaled the helicopter back after they had completed their eighth lap.

In the 45 minutes since the helicopter had arrived, a rain squall came in. It started raining and the wind began to blow much harder. The guys on the rocks told me to "enjoy the ride" in the basket. That was not going to happen because I am afraid of heights.

The helicopter was creating hurricane force winds from the propeller. As a parting thought, Ben told me, "Look up and enjoy the ride". I said, "No" because I was scared and tired. On top of that, according to Wikipedia, "these (Stokes) baskets are notorious for spinning under the downdraft from the rotating helicopter blades." I can confirm this is true.

I closed my eyes as the cable lifted me and the basket the 100+ feet to the helicopter. There is a video taken by the Coast Guard cutter of my ascent. Curren is holding onto the trail line to keep me from spinning too much. But I am going back-and-forth quite a bit. The rain is coming down hard.

The basket comes up directly under the aircraft. To get it into the helicopter, Beau had to manually lift it in. To do this, he is strapped into the helicopter, laying on his stomach. He pushed the basket slightly away from the helicopter, lifted it up, and pulled the basket into the bay of the helicopter. This requires him to lift a 160-pound person, along with the weight of the basket and wrangle in a rain storm with a lot of wind. Beau looked down at me and thought to himself, "He is in rough shape and in shock. I could tell he was frightened." He said to me, "I got you, man."

With me in the helicopter, they lowered the cable with a hook to bring Curren back to join us. Before taking off for the airport, the crew had one more checklist to do. Beau led them through some important things, like making sure the door is closed and everything was secured in the helicopter. While those may appear to be simple things, the Coast Guard has learned that just when things seem okay is when problems can occur. Taking a few moments to ensure everything is in order is part of the discipline that makes the Coast Guard so effective.

* * * *

Down on the rocks, Jason summed up the situation for the whole rescue team, "I usually do not get emotional on calls; however, when the victim was safely raised in the litter, a sigh of relief came over all the rescuers and myself."

Rose and Stephen had small snippets of information. Every time the helicopter flew away, they were afraid the helicopter was abandoning the mission. Rose said, "We saw the rescue swimmer lowered to the rocks. We took that as a good sign. Then it seemed like an eternity waiting for the next step."

Finally, when they saw me lifted away from the rocks, they knew they could exhale.

"I don't know if I have ever cried that hard. Ever," Stephen recalled. "Just holding onto mom. Squeezing each other. We were both shaking and crying because now dad has a better shot at living." Soon thereafter was the third time Stephen was throwing up.

"As rescuers arrived back at the beach and rides were assigned, each of them had something to say to me," Rose recalled. "Malik gave me his St. Croix FD shirt for Dean. He said he promised it to Dean when they were out on the rocks as a remembrance. I clutched it to my chest as if it was an heirloom to be remembered forever."

"Karl told me he never left Dean once he found him. "He said, Dean's first words when he got out of the hole were Where's Rose? Dean was worried about you. When you see him, you be happy. He needs you to be strong. I hugged Devron, Malik, and Karl so hard. I didn't know If I would ever see them again. I knew I would be eternally grateful to these men."

Stephen and Rose would not hike back to the car because that would be another two miles of walking. They rode in Ben's jeep back to their car. Stephen was in the back part without a seat and got banged around quite a bit. The road into and out of the tide pools took 40 minutes to get back to the parking lot.

Once they arrived back at the car, Stephen had no internet connection on his phone. Therefore, they had no GPS to get directions to the hospital. So, Jason volunteered to lead them to the hospital. Stephen told Rose he had gathered phone numbers for John and Amie, Ben, and Jason. She couldn't believe he had the foresight to get phone numbers. But that was just Stephen being Stephen.

* * * *

In the five-minute helicopter ride to the airport, I did not say much. Curren pulled out a wool blanket to try to warm me. He did not have any time to attend to my cuts, because it was a short ride to the hospital.

Co-pilot Billy had been communicating with the airport. He made sure they knew when the helicopter was coming and that it was an emergency. The airport needed to make sure no commercial or private aircraft would be landing or taking off. The Command Center was making sure an ambulance would be ready for me.

The trip to the airport went by as a blur. I don't remember a thing; I did not say anything to the helicopter crew. Upon landing, Curren and Beau carried me out and put me in the ambulance. I was now off to the hospital.

I had made it through the most harrowing ordeal of my life. But that day was far from over. It was now time for me to get assessed at the hospital and begin the journey to recovery.

A postscript

When we went back to Puerto Rico in June 2023 (seven months after the incident) to visit, it was a very emotional talk with the helicopter crew. They were gracious with their time. They were moved by our willingness to come say thank you.

"This (being part of a rescue mission) is what I've wanted to do since I was in high school," Billy told us.

Curren added, "It was definitely rewarding to actually be able to do what we were able to do for you. It is even more rewarding having you here face-to-face now. It could have not turned out that way. It happens too often. You being alive and visiting us is meaningful."

Beau and Billy told us they were on a rescue mission the week before we arrived. Unfortunately, that person did not survive. Such is the life of a Coast Guard service member.

Chapter 10: Why Did I Survive?

"I think one of the most important, and difficult, challenges of . . . life in general-is striking a balance between focusing your attention on what's right in front of you and remaining open to new possibilities."
David Epstein

I've spent a lot of time wondering "why did I survive". When you have a near death experience, you join a fraternity of a small population. Many others don't survive. It's generally not their fault. It is natural to have bit of survivor's guilt. I feel it is important to explore some reasons why I was saved.

My best guess is that it is a combination of three things that all worked together: me, the rescuers and healthcare professionals, and divine intervention. My survival is built on a series of deliberate choices made by each of us at moments in our life, both long ago and recently.

#1. My Role.

I am not comfortable with people telling me I am amazing for surviving; however, I understand now that it is an important part of the narrative. I may not like the attention, nor do I want to brag. I am not more extraordinary than other people. However, choices I have made throughout my life put me in the position to have a hand in my survival.

Down in the hole, the combination of mental and physical fortitude was necessary. The mental part was the first key. I don't ever remember panicking. I was present in the moment. While reality was very clear to me, it did not defeat me.

I realize that the years I have spent running prepared me for this moment, physically and mentally. Anyone who has known me for long knows I use running as much for my mental health as I do for my physical health. When I worked at NCR Corporation many years ago, my team leaders would tell me to "go for a run, you are getting crabby". They knew I was a much better leader and thinker after I had run.

A runner's mind also knows that each run is a part of a longer processes. Getting caught up in comparing today's run to one in the past or the goal for the future run is not a way to prepare. A runner needs to be present to today's run and adjust accordingly. I realize that my mind is conditioned for that.

I am convinced that this training has educated my mind and body how to work differently. I have learned how to endure a little more discomfort than I thought was possible. Without consciously thinking about it, that probably played a positive role in my situation.

I am in better physical shape than most people my age. Starting from a strong position meant that my physical degradation, while bad, was not as dangerous as it was for others who might not be in my healthy condition. We all read and hear about the need for physical exercise. Yet few choose to take the time to do it. I made that choice long ago and stuck with it.

It is interesting to reflect that I have never made the decision to exercise and be healthy as preparation for being in a near-death experience. None of us think that way. But it worked out that was an outcome of my physical health.

#2 The selfless acts of "ordinary people" were vitally important.

A big part of the story for me is that ordinary people stepped up and did what was necessary. Presented with a horrible situation, they took action. Immediately.

John and Amie were there with a cell phone to call 911. They stuck on the phone with the 911 dispatchers to get information across. They remained on the scene as long as they could, providing moral support.

Karl and Devron were doing their day job as tour guides, but once they encountered Rose, they understood they might be able to make a difference. They did not hesitate to act

Karl was willing to stick his head into a hole in the volcanic rock, even though water would rise up in the hole, to ensure the best chance of me hearing him. Once we connected via voice, he continued to engage me for the next 20 minutes while we waited for the rope and the chance to pull me out.

Ben happened to be driving to the tide pools that day to take his brother and his brother's girlfriend to see the pools. He decided to throw his rescue rope into his jeep. Without that rope, they probably would not have gotten me out of the hole.

Once the other three rescuers came onto the scene (Jason, Malik, and Shumba), all six of them had roles to play. They gave the shirts off their back and secured the towels that covered me. I don't know if any of them ever got those items back.

Until the helicopter arrived and whisked me away, those six individuals stayed with me on the rocks. Despite the fact that they had never worked together before, and were all trained differently, they were a team.

I was the fortunate recipient of a well-trained helicopter crew. Having never done a mission together before, Travis, Billy, Beau, and Curren meshed to pull off a very tough rescue operation.

The years 2020-2022 were very hard for hospital workers due to the COVID-19 Pandemic. Long hours. Lack of resources. Unprecedented deaths. The Great Resignation. Being whiplashed from "heroes" to "villains" based on the requirements for vaccines, masks, and other safety protocols. When I needed the services of well-trained, concerned individuals, they served me.

I think it is also safe to say that many people would be concerned with having to go to a hospital in a small Caribbean Island with a life-threatening situation. I did not have a choice of course. However, the professionalism and the care of the people who watched over me was fantastic.

#3 Divine Intervention

I am not one to believe that I was purposely selected by God to be saved. I am uncomfortable with that mainly because it makes me more special in God's eyes than other people. I do not believe that I am special. When I tell the story of my rescue, I acknowledge the "miracles" that happened. Two people, who were experts on every inch of the tide pools show up. Ben sticks the rope in his vehicle for the first time in a year. The rope manages to float to me when Ben threw it down the hole on the first try. There were no other pressing emergencies, therefore the helicopter could be dispatched to pull me off the rocks.

Too many miracles for this to be a series of random events. I may have made some of my own luck, but I got a lot of help along the way.

Without all three of those things happening—my fortitude, the rescuers doing their part, and some miracles—I probably don't write these words. Each of us gets the power to decide which of these three sticks out to them. But I know that all of them were critical.

RECOVERY

Chapter 11: Emergency Department

"In all affairs it's a healthy thing now and then to hang a question mark on the things you take for granted." Bertrand Russell

I was back on solid ground. Curren and Beau got me out of the helicopter on the board I was on and delivered me to the ambulance. The helicopter crew had done their job. I was taken immediately to Governor Juan Luis Hospital where I met the next set of heroes in my recovery.

I arrived around 5:00 p.m. It had been nearly five hours since I was first sucked into the hole at the tide pools. The first thing was to do a full assessment of my health (ROS or Review of Systems, in hospital talk). The readings from the rocks were indicators, but not as accurate as in the hospital. The Emergency Department (ED) has a set of protocols to follow.

Luckily for me, another "coincidence" put me in the hands of an expert, Dr. Lauren Bacon, who is an ED doctor who specializes in disasters. She was only in St. Croix for two weeks because she had been sent there as part of the training for her disaster specialty program. The only reason she was working that Tuesday night was because she had moved shifts later in the week around to have a few days off to rest, relax, and visit the Island.

Dr. Bacon knew of my situation from the early calls but was busy in the afternoon attending to other patients in the ED. During a lull in activity, she checked on the status from the tide pools. In the confusion of the early reports, they did not know if I was submerged underwater, not getting any oxygen to my brain or if I was trapped but breathing.

"Once I got word that the victim was at the airport and arriving soon, we prepared for his arrival," Dr. Bacon recollected. "He was now going to be my patient; in my care and the care of an ED staff I barely knew but trusted. I took the reports of the victim's ability to communicate on the scene as an indicator that his condition was perhaps better than first imagined."

To address the most obvious issues, I was immediately put on oxygen and an external device that blew hot air under my blankets to warm my body. Having a heater warming me felt so good.

They also did CT scans and blood work. They quickly found out, perhaps to their surprise, that I did not have a lot of serious physical injuries. I had no broken bones. No internal injuries. No concussion. Despite having bad scrapes on 75% of my body, there were no major cuts. The only items that had to be addressed were a couple deep cuts on my head (from being banged against the rocks). I ended up with six small staples in my head.

After getting the tests and making the assessments, the health care team (Dr, Joseph, Dr. Blankensmith, and Dr Bacon, nurses Tim Cordell and Cadira McIntosh and respiratory therapist Amanda Crossland) began attending me. They had a number of immediate concerns.

The first concern was my breathing and the state of my lungs. The oxygen from the tank that Ben had with him and brought to the rocks was very helpful. My blood oxygen level read at 99 when I got to the ED. This was a major surprise, and a good one. I had not suffered a loss of oxygen that could have been very detrimental to the rest of my body, especially my brain.

Dr. Bacon told me when I spoke with her months later, "You were doing really, really well considering everything. To this day I am surprised that mentally you were not in a vegetative state, delay, or memory loss. Your memory was good. You had some confusion about where your family was, but that was understandable. Overall, you were doing surprisingly well."

My lungs were in bad shape due to all of the salt water I swallowed. My breathing was shallow and labored. One number gives an indicator of how weak my breathing was. Normally, we take 12-17 breaths per minute. A rate over 24 breaths per minute indicates a very serious condition. I was at 44 breaths per minute on the rocks, nearly double "very serious condition". I was gasping for breath. Upon arrival at the ED, my rate was 36, still concerningly high.

The 6:24 p.m. CT scan of my lungs showed that I had a partial collapse of my right lung, along with fluid in both lungs. This needed to be addressed quickly to avoid pneumonia and further damage to my lungs.

The second concern was my blood sodium level, which registered at 161. The normal blood sodium level is 135 to 145 milliequivalents/liter. This meant I was hypernatremic, too much sodium in the bloodstream. I was displaying typical symptoms of this: muscle weakness, restlessness, extreme thirst, confusion, lethargy, and irritability.

The most worrying complication of hypernatremia is the risk of water loss in brain cells, causing them to shrink, which could cause a cerebral hemorrhage leading to permanent brain damage or death. The protocol is to carefully lower my sodium levels, because doing it too fast or too slowly would increase the chance of complications.

"When we got your labs came back, your sodium was through the roof (161). I have never seen a number that high in my life," Dr. Bacon remarked. "That told me you swallowed so much sea water. There is no other way to get at number that high. I have seen a lot of dehydrated patients, but never anyone with a number that high. Your body was doing everything to get rid of the sodium."

Unfortunately for me, my hypernatremia meant I was not going to be allowed to drink any liquids. We could not put more liquids into me until we got my sodium a little more under control. I would eventually go nearly 24 hours without drinking anything.

The third concern was to mitigate the risk of infection in all of the abrasions. The only parts of my body without cuts were my face and my chest. Lying in bed covered in blankets, I might not have looked bad. But looking at my back, they could see I had so many cuts. Between the sea water and the particles from the rock, there was concern about infection.

The fourth concern was with "secondary drowning", a dangerous complication of a drowning close call that can develop up to 48 hours later. This most often happens if water gets into the lungs. When in the lungs, the water can irritate the lungs' lining and fluid can build up. When there is a large amount of fluid in the lungs, it can limit the lungs' ability to properly inflate and oxygenate the blood, sometimes to the point of respiratory failure.

Fifth was my electrolyte (sodium, calcium, potassium, chlorine, phosphate, and magnesium) imbalance. Electrolytes help your body's blood chemistry, muscle action, electrical stimulation, and other processes. When the electrolytes are out-of-balance, like mine were, there is a greater risk for heart attack or stroke.

Lastly, my vital signs showed how out of whack my body was. My blood pressure was 188/92 (normal is 120/80). My pulse rate was 122; my normal pulse rate is in the 50s. They needed to be monitored continually.

Only the medical professionals understood how many things could go wrong to cause permanent damage. I was in no condition to understand them. We did not know how high I was at risk of stroke, cerebral hemorrhage, pneumonia, etc.

* * * *

Rose and Stephen entered the ED in their bathing suits at around 6:00 p.m. Stephen did not have on a shirt. All he had was a swim suit and shoes. His legs, shoes, and arms were covered in blood. They walked up to the ER desk and the person there naturally thought Stephen was there for treatment. Once the desk understood the two of them were there for me, a doctor talked to them.

"I did not remember much of that discussion," Rose remembers. "My mind was solely focused on getting to see Dean to verify he was alive. It still was not real to me that he survived. We also did not entirely understand the extent of his condition. How could we?"

I was conscious when Rose and Stephen arrived. It was so good to see them healthy and alive. Up until that moment, I had no idea of their fate. Tears formed in my eyes when Rose came close to me.

Rose recalled upon seeing me, "Dean's chest area was the only area that looked unharmed. I went to his right side and laid my hand there on his chest. It felt so important to touch him and be connected to him." Stephen was comforted by the fact that I recognized them when I arrived. That let him know I was okay mentally.

I was on oxygen, still shivering, and was not myself much of the time. I could talk to them, but not clearly. I would be in the middle of a conversation and then I would float away mentally.

None of my vital numbers were good, but I didn't understand how bad or what the dangers were yet. Just like on the rocks, my numbers indicated I was in bad shape, but since I was talking, conscious, and responsive everyone took those things as good signs.

One of the first things I told them was that I was thirsty and wanted a drink. This would become a recurring theme throughout the night.

"From my perspective, the worst sign was Dean's mental state of unreasonableness," Rose went on, "He wanted a drink badly and no matter how we explained it was dangerous, he was insistent. At one point in the evening, Stephen left a Diet Coke cup he had been drinking. Dean saw the drink and asked me for it. Dean does not drink soda. Ever. He didn't care if it was soda or not because he was that thirsty. WhenI said, 'No you cannot have it'. He said back to me, 'Ro, if you don't give me a drink, I will hate you forever.' I replied, 'I hope that's a long time.' He was not thinking very clearly."

I don't remember that exchange. But Rose lived it. There are so many out-of-character elements to it. I realize that was a good summation of my psychological state for all of the first night in the hospital.

Stephen realized his mom was going to be focused solely on her husband. He took it upon himself to be the action guy asking most of the questions of the healthcare workers. Having a mission felt better.

Amanda Crossland was my respiratory therapist in the ED. She was a blessing. Professional, caring, and informative, she was the most memorable person for me in the ED. I was so out of it mentally; I could not remember a lot from the ED. Because of the very large concern that I could be impacted by a secondary drowning ("dry drowning"), Amanda needed to keep a sharp eye on me. We spent a lot of time together.

Her job was critically important, because my lungs were one of the most damaged parts of my body. In order to get more accurate data about my respiratory system, she needed to insert a stent to get an arterial blood reading of my blood oxygen level. Amanda tried a number of times to get the stent in, to no avail. My arteries kept collapsing because I was so dehydrated.

Even though she could not get the stent in, she could make an assessment. Her observation was that my numbers were not great, indicating I was in a serious condition. However, my communication, my being myself (at times), even my ornery attitude about wanting water, told her everything she needed to know about my condition. I was fighting to get better fast.

Amanda and I remembered the same story. She told me early in our interaction, "I am the person you are going to hate." She knew the stent and the BiPap mask were not going to be popular items with me. As she told me later, "I don't see people on their good day."

The next thing she had to administer was a nasogastric intubation tube up my nose and down my esophagus into my stomach in order to pump my stomach. Dr. Bacon had noted that my stomach sounded like a drum because it had so much water in it. The tube was going to get that out of me.

"Your stomach. I was really taken aback how bloated your stomach was," Dr. Bacon remembered, "You were filled with water in every sense. Stomach and lungs. I did not need a stethoscope. You had water everywhere in your body. We needed to get that out of your stomach." Stephen characterized my stomach as looking like I had two bowling balls inside me.

Once the tube was in, they could put me on a BiPap machine.

The BiPap machine has a "Darth Vader" like mask connected to a ventilator that pushes air into my lungs. The BiPap machine basically helped open my lungs with air pressure. This was a major first step in getting my breathing back to normal. The BiPap mask came with its downsides. It was uncomfortable. It made speaking communication from me nearly impossible.

Amanda was great in explaining the whole procedure to self-repair my lungs. She described aspiration of the lungs and my alveoli, the small sacs in a patient's lungs that transfer oxygen from the lungs to the capillaries to get into your blood. The alveoli are rounded at the bottom and there is a protein at the bottom (surfactant) that was washed away by the salt water. Surfactant is released from the lung cells and spreads across the tissue that surrounds alveoli. This substance lowers surface tension, which keeps the alveoli from collapsing after exhalation and makes breathing easy.

With my alveoli deflated and the surfactant washed away, my body needed the time and space to rebuild. Getting the water out of my lungs and pumping pure oxygen into my lungs was the best way to do this. The BiPap machine was forcing the alveoli process while allowing them time to self-repair.

I understand now the BiPap machine would get my lungs working again, but that wasn't my concern at the time. The machine and the tube in my nose and throat had me focused on how dry my mouth was.

I was not a very friendly patient. It did not matter who entered the room, I would ask them for some water to drink. When they would not give it to me, I told each of them that I did not like them. This went on for more than 10 hours. I don't know how everyone put up with me, other than the fact they are used to it.

At some later point, Amanda gave me my first mouth swab. Just being able to taste and suck on a sponge with a minimal amount of liquid was so great for my mouth. That is when I told her that "I liked her".

"You bounced back way faster than anyone I have seen in that scenario. It was miraculous," Amanda told me later. "It is absolutely amazing; everything had to line up just right for you to be here."

Rose recalled from the early part of the evening a story that summed up how I was. "Dean kept telling the nurses and doctors that if he could just get up and walk around a little bit, he would feel better and get better faster. Dean is not a person that sits around ever for very long (he got that from his mother). He did not understand how bad his condition was."

Rose continued. "You don't understand, I know myself," Dean would say. "I don't stay still at home. If I could just get up and walk a little, it will help me get better. Doctors, nurses, and respiratory therapists said 'no' to him several times in several different ways. Dean kept asking, being unreasonable and that wasn't like him normally. "

"Finally, Dr. Bacon said he could stand next to his bed and while holding on, he could walk from one end of the bed to the other. Dean thanked her. It was clear he was grateful and felt heard. He never got to do what Dr. Bacon mentioned, but he never asked again. She understood that it was listening to him and coming up with a solution that was important."

* * * *

I remember asking Rose and Stephen numerous times about "my numbers". Because the blood pressure reading, heart rate, etc. were on a monitor behind my head, I could not see them. Tracking my numbers' status was one way to understand how I was doing. They told me what the numbers said. We all knew they were not good. Anytime something showed an improvement, it felt like a success, however small.

Laying in a hospital ED bed with my mouth covered, having oxygen pumped into me, and a tube down my throat was not something I have ever experienced. I was so weak and so disoriented.

Reflecting back on the ordeal of the day, it is hard to imagine the toll it took on Rose and Stephen. Rose and Stephen were with me that long day and night. I can only speculate on their mental state. They had gone from acknowledging that I was dead, to hearing I was alive (but not able to see me), to watching the four hours of rescue operations from afar, and finally seeing me leaving via helicopter. Seeing me in the ED was their first opportunity to see how badly I was injured, but at least I was alive. The two of them spent a long night with me and the healthcare professionals trying to stabilize me.

Once we "settled in", we watched my numbers, sought information from the doctors and nurses, and did whatever they could to help me. At some point in time, I told Rose and Stephen about how sore my feet were from the scrapes on them. For a while, one or the other held my feet and propped them up on a pillow to relieve the pain.

Between the BiPap mask and the tube, I was uncomfortable, getting more dehydrated, and could barely communicate.

Amanda, the respiratory therapist told me, "I checked in on you a lot. I asked questions like, Does your throat hurt? Are you having any trouble breathing? Those would be signs of dry drowning. As long as you were complaining about wanting water, it was good. Sometimes complaining is not a bad thing. I like it when my patients are feisty, it tells me you are fighting to get better."

When I wanted to say something, I needed to make eye contact with someone. Then I tried to say a few words. It often did not work. Luckily, Amanda and Stephen got quite good at translating my "mask voice" into a real voice (Amanda called it "BiPapeze" language). They were my voice to the outside world. It is impossible to overstate how important it was to have someone who "understood me" when the rest of the world did not. It was one way of easing my distressed state.

One important note about the hospital is that it had been severely damaged by two category 5 hurricanes in 2017. Since St. Croix is a US territory, you might think it could get funds to fix the hospital. It could not. While the hospital is a three-story building, the third floor was condemned due to water damage. In addition, the first-floor restrooms were not operational. That led to another funny story for the evening.

I had to go the bathroom badly. I asked if I could walk to the bathroom. I assumed there was a bathroom in my room. I would have been required to walk outside to a port-a-john. I did not have the strength to get out of bed, let alone walk somewhere. But I did not understand that at all. Rose coaxed me to go into a small bottle-like device the hospital had. Humiliating to say the least. But it was the best we could do.

There was another solution to that problem. I got a catheter inserted. This procedure can be described in one word. Pain. Since I was not allowed to get out of bed, it was the only way to go to the bathroom. It also allowed the healthcare professionals to more easily collect my urine to do testing. Memorable, but not fun.

Around 8:00 p.m., the most painful event of the hospital stay (more painful than the catheter insertion) occurred. They had to clean all of my wounds with hydrogen peroxide in order to protect against infection. The three of them—Nurse Cadira, Rose, and Stephen—had to work together. I did not have the strength to roll onto one side or the other. They had to roll me over. Cadira used a sponge with hydrogen peroxide all over my back. Then they rolled me onto my other side. This was the most intense, painful experience. It was agony. I allowed myself to scream in pain. Rose said I was certainly not stoic at that time.

After things settled down a bit, it became a long night in the hospital. The minutes seemed to move slowly. At times, I was coherent. At others, I was not. Rose wondered if that was normal for my condition or had I suffered some long-lasting impact?

"My thoughts were focused on staying positive and strong for Dean and Stephen," Rose recalled. "I remembered what Karl had told me about being positive and supportive of Dean. I believe Stephen had much the same mindset. We wanted to keep clear heads so we could understand information from the doctors and nurses."

"No-one told us that Dean was in immediate danger. They did tell us that they had to get the salt water out of his lungs and stomach. We understood his salt levels were dangerously high and needed to be brought back in line slowly or it could result in brain bleed, seizure, or death. We knew all that. We just stayed positive and trusted them."

During the night, one of the rescuers, Devron, visited us in the ED briefly. I was not awake, but Stephen and Rose were so grateful to see him.

The Intensive Care Unit (ICU) doctor came in to see me around 3:00 a.m. Wednesday morning. He said he would admit me since I was stabilized. He did not offer a prognosis. He just explained everything they were doing.

I slept, fitfully, for brief moments of time throughout the night. The hours dragged on. Somewhere around 4:00 a.m. on Wednesday, November 23, we began the discussion with the ED team to take me to the ICU. As part of this discussion, the plan to put a central port (aka "Central Line") in me was brought up. I got the gist of the procedure. However, I was only receiving the "good" reasons for doing it and then was asked to approve that procedure.

I was lucid enough to not be comfortable with that little amount of information. I looked with wide eyes at Stephen to signal him I had something to say. I wanted to hear the good news and bad news. What were possible complications? Stephen got my concerns immediately. He relayed my wishes and told them we were not going to decide without hearing both sides. They told us all that might happen, which Stephen summarized. We decide to go forward. At the time we were leaving the ED, they were going to put the port in my thigh/leg.

Rose remembers thinking, Dean balked at the central line without knowing all the details, he is being VERY REASONABLE; that is a good sign of his mental state.

A central line (also called a central venous catheter) is like an intravenous (IV) line. But it is much longer than a regular IV and goes all the way to a vein near the heart or just inside the heart. It would make it easy to provide me with medicine, fluids, and nutrition all at the same time. It would also be used to draw blood. We were going to use a three-line port: 1 line for hydration, 1 line for antibiotics, and 1 line for drawing blood.

If that was going to heal me faster, I was all for it.

Chapter 12: Family Arrives/ICU, Wednesday, November 23

"Days may not be fair, always

That's when I'll be there, always

Not for just an hour

Not for just a day

Not for just a year, but, always" Irving Berlin, "Always"

Around 4:15 a.m., I was wheeled up to the ICU. Rose and Stephen were not allowed to come, so they drove back to the house. They left knowing I was not better, but I was not any worse. Driving home, Rose remembered saying to Stephen, "I can't believe this day really happened; all of it."

Wednesday was an important day because the rest of our family, Courtney, Nate and Amanda, and Luke were going to arrive at different times. Rose and Stephen had made the decision not tell them of the day's events because of the unknown prognosis. We did not have enough specific information to tell people. When those two last saw me, I was stable, but my long-term prognosis was unknown as I headed to the ICU. Who knew what would happen in the intervening six hours?

Stephen offered to pick up our daughter, Courtney, at the airport at 8:30 a.m. Rose should just sleep in.

Rose sent a text to the rest of our children from my phone trying to sound like me (whatever that means), writing 'text your dad with any flight changes.' Stephen went to get Courtney while Rose ordered Thanksgiving dinner from the local grocery. Waiting with nothing else to do until they could go to the ICU at 10:00, she did anything she could to distract her mind.

As Stephen drove the 20 minutes to the airport, he had time to reflect. He was cut up very badly and had not done much to fix the wounds. With only three hours of sleep, he was exhausted. He and his mom had been through an excruciating afternoon and evening. Now he was going to be charge of telling the rest of the family what had happen and what he knew. It was not going to be easy.

Courtney had taken a red-eye flight from New York City and was due in around 9:00 a.m. Nate and his wife, Amanda, were scheduled for a 5:00 p.m. arrival. Our youngest, Luke, was scheduled an hour later. It was going to fall to Stephen to tell each one of his siblings an abridged version of the story and my current condition, having not had a chance to make sense of it all.

Courtney's plane arrived on time and she knew Stephen was going to pick her up. She did not think twice about why her Mom and Dad were not greeting her. As she greeted Stephen, she said in a joking manner, "How has it been with Mom and Dad for the last 36 hours (joking that it had to be bad)?" Stephen crumbled to the ground and started sobbing.

"I could not imagine what had happened. That was not the reaction I was expecting," Courtney thought. "What could possibly be that bad that he reacts this way? What did I just stumble into?" Stephen was fighting tears as he tried to choke out a message. He got across to her that her dad was in the hospital and "I do not know how he is alive".

She got snippets of the story from Stephen's perspective while they were driving to the house to pick up Rose. She remembers him telling her about some of the miracles that occurred in the rescue. He told her about yelling to his mom, "I am going to die" and she helped save him. Courtney learned about the areas of concern with her dad and the current trends. She did not question anything, recognizing how distraught Stephen was. She found herself stunned by all she heard and was struggling to process it coherently.

"I remember looking at Stephen and saw how badly thrashed his legs were. Cuts, marks, scrapes everywhere," Courtney pondered. "I could not take all of this in. It was overwhelming, considering I had flown all night and was looking forward to a relaxing, fun family vacation. I struggled to wrap my head around my dad being almost dead. My perspective was that dad is recovering."

They drove back to the house to pick up Rose, who was so relieved to be hugged by Courtney. She relayed how Stephen had broken down when he told her of dad's ordeal. She told Rose, "Mom, it's awful, but I didn't have to live through it. I'm here for you and Stephen now. Whatever you need."

Rose had a list of things that needed to be done (pay for Thanksgiving dinner, get some medicine for Stephen, find my medical insurance card). They left quickly for the hospital. They stopped at the grocer to prepay Thanksgiving dinner. Rose was thinking, "Our original vacation plan was out the door, but I was determined that we would have a family dinner."

Courtney looked at her phone and realized "it's now 10:00 and we are not yet at the hospital. Mom and Stephen were agitated that they were late. That gave me an insight into how nervous and on-edge the two of them were. I knew I needed to be a rock for them and help however I could. Mom had to talk to the hospital's financial office about Dad's medical insurance, so I decided to stay with her."

Stephen went immediately up to the ICU.

* * * *

The doctor originally was going to insert the central line in my leg, using the femoral artery. I honestly don't know why, but the decision was made to place it in the internal jugular, on the left side of my neck. It was around 5:00 a.m. on Wednesday, November 23.

I was awake as the doctor did this procedure. Amanda, my respiratory therapist from the ED, was assisting the doctor. It was nice to have her familiar voice in the room. She draped a cloth over my neck and head. The doctor numbed a part of my neck to insert the line. It took maybe 15 minutes to do this relatively simple procedure (open up a small spot and get three thin wires into me). The doctor told Amanda that one artery after another collapsed due to my dehydration. When I heard he had the one in near my heart, I was concerned that something was going wrong. But that is the way it is supposed to work.

With the line now in me, I was wheeled to my new "home", the second door on the left in the ICU.

The set of lines made my care much easier. I was now receiving fluids through an IV. I still had not been allowed to drink anything for nearly 18 hours at this time. But getting fluids meant my dehydration would start to diminish. Also, I no longer had to be poked and prodded to find a vein or artery for blood draws.

I settled into the ICU hospital routine. A number of specialists visited me at different points throughout the morning. A breathing treatment started to help clear my lungs and ward off infection. An aide came in periodically to empty and test the contents of the bag from the catheter. Someone else would take some of my blood for testing. Of course, the machines would start beeping periodically when an IV bag needed replacing. Sleep was fitful at best.

At 7:57 a.m. I was awakened to have an EKG done by technician, Wes. He was a nice guy, originally from the American Southwest. Just like every other person who came to treat me, I asked his name and engaged with him. He put me through the EKG process. While Wes could not give me the official prognosis, he did tell me that from what he knows, my heart looked good. A great sign, no heart damage.

Every time someone came in to test me or check a number, I asked them what the results were. I was starved for information. I guess being trapped alone in that cavern made me desperately crave connection with everyone I came in contact with. I gathered as much information as I could.

Steve Chmura was my Wednesday ICU nurse from 7:30 a.m.–7:30 p.m. Steve's presence was another very lucky circumstance in a long string of good fortune. Steve is an ED nurse normally. However, he was on a rotation, substituting in the ICU for another person for a couple weeks. Having him for 12 hours was a great joy. He was incredibly patient and articulate. As I started to get rapidly better with the introduction of antibiotics, IV fluids, and oxygen, my family and I had a million questions. He patiently answered them all.

Grace Kim was my ICU respiratory therapist. She had to continually check my blood oxygen levels and respiration rate. I connected with Grace very quickly. I knew how important her role was in my condition. Like everyone else, I wanted to know her name, and what she was looking for in me. I have no idea if I was bothersome or inquisitive, but Grace emulated her name. She made me feel calmer and I knew I was in good hands.

She saw the immediate improvement from the numbers I had in the ED. When I woke up Wednesday morning, the decision to wean me off the BiPap machine had been made, as long as I continued improvement. She told me we were going to try four hours on the BiPap machine, then oxygen mask for four hours, and then back on the BiPap machine for four more hours. At 10:30 a.m. on Wednesday, she came to take me off the BiPap machine. I remember the time because that BiPap machine was so restricting. I could now communicate more clearly.

I asked Grace if I could go without the oxygen mask for my four-hour break. It would make communicating with family better. It would also be a good test of my lung capacity. Grace agreed to give it a try. I believe this is a sign of an excellent medical professional: one who listens. When she came to see me two hours later, I was still at a good blood oxygen level of 99. She told me, 'Your blood oxygen level is better than mine.'

It had been 24 hours since I was sucked underwater, and already my respiratory system was doing much better. That was highly encouraging.

* * * *

Rose and Courtney finished with the medial insurance card. Security needed to see their COVID vaccination cards, which they had. The ICU has a rule of one visitor per room, but they did not enforce it on our family. We were so thankful for that. They joined Stephen in my room.

On seeing me, Courtney recalled, "I have never seen my dad in a hospital bed. My dad started tearing up. He looked so feeble in that hospital bed. A lot of emotions were going on as this is the first time that we saw each other since the incident. I put my hand on dad's arm to make physical contact."

Nurse Steve came in and told us what was going on. He patiently explained the situation. Most importantly, my blood sodium level had dropped to 153 (the goal is 145). Vital signs were stabilizing.

However, Courtney noticed that I was still not myself. I slurred my words and sometimes couldn't seem to find the right words to say. My communication was not great.

Rose was relieved to see that I was clearly doing much better. I had a small sponge on a stick that looked like a lollipop. I could dip it in ice water and suck on it every so often. It felt so good to have a little liquid. I wasn't allowed to overdo it. Rose thought, "one sign that Dean was getting better was that he was following that direction. He only asked for it once every 30-45 minutes."

Around noon, Courtney and Stephen left to go back to the house to get some sleep. I slept fitfully. It was so cold in the ICU; I wanted blankets covering all parts of my body. Rose stayed with me and tried to sleep in the chair with a bunch of blankets on her.

Two hours later, we put the BiPap machine back on as planned, but Grace promised to come back around 4:30 (halfway through my next four-hour stint) to check on me. At the rate I was improving, she said if I continued, she would pull me off two hours early. As promised, she came back two hours later. Upon her return, she assessed that I was doing well. She made the decision to pull me off the Bipap machine.

That was another big step in a number of ways. First, it meant I was recovering well. Second, without the machine, I could communicate normally.

Courtney and Stephen returned around 2:30 p.m. When they came back, I was livelier and wanted to communicate. At first, I had the BiPap mask on, but it was not for long. Rose left to try to nap more comfortably in the ICU waiting room.

Nurse Steve continued to be great at providing status on my numbers. In the nine hours between 5:10 a.m. and 2:40 p.m., my blood sodium level only reduced from 153 to 151. I was disappointed, but Steve assured me that is exactly what we wanted to happen. The sodium levels needed to come down slowly, allowing my body to readjust and get rid of the excess sodium in a controlled manner. Not knowing better, I wanted everything to be "good" quickly. Steve assured me this was the best path for my dangerous sodium levels.

Around 4:00, Stephen and Rose left to pick up Nate and Amanda at the airport. Courtney stayed with me. She was there when they took the Nasogastric Tube out of my nose. Steve, the nurse, told us this was another good thing and a sign of my progress. I was excited that this was going to happen because it would make swallowing and communication even easier.

Steve told me, "This is going to hurt a little bit because I had the tube taped around your nose." He started yanking out the tube. I don't exactly remember my reaction, other than feeling this thing getting pulled through my nose. Courtney was stunned by how much tubing come out. As she recalled, it looked like "three feet" of tube was pulled out of me through my nose. I imagine it looked like a magician pulling a seemingly endless string of things out of a hat. I was relieved when it was all over.

With that tube out, I was now allowed to have something to drink. This was a huge moment. Nearly 24 hours after first arriving at the hospital, I was about to have my first sip of anything. Nurse Steve came back with some iced tea in a cup. I was required to sip slowly. I took my time. I told Courtney, "That is the blandest tea I ever had and the best tea I have ever had." I was now becoming much more like myself in her eyes.

Courtney took a picture of the bad scrape on my forehead. It looked like I had head butted someone. I did not even know it was there until she showed it to me. Because she had not seen them, I showed her the cuts and scrapes on my legs. She saw that I was scraped up much worse than Stephen.

The other key with the tube out was I was going to be allowed to eat soon. To supplement the hospital food, Stephen and Rose were going to pick up yogurt and applesauce at the grocery store.

Nurse Steve was able to articulate to us part of the reason he believed I got so much better so quickly. As he got to know me, he understood I am a runner (I run about 30 miles a week). He learned that I raced half marathons. In his eyes, my recovery made a little more sense knowing that information. He noted that when I run a race, I push my body to its fullest. I stress my systems. My brain and body work together to allow me to run beyond limits they would prefer. Once the race is over, my body knows it is time to recuperate. I have to flush out lactic acid. Blood flows throughout my body to move tissue and muscle damage out. My kidneys process everything. He believes that training kicked in here also.

Stephen and Rose left to pick up our son and daughter-in-law, Nate and Amanda, at the airport. Stephen dropped Rose off and went to park the car. Rose ran into Nate and Amanda near baggage claim.

Rose reflected on their meeting.

"There is often humor in dark times. As Nathan and Amanda got off their airplane, Amanda went to look for their luggage. Nathan immediately got on his phone to check the University of Dayton (UD) basketball score. We (Nate and Rose) are season ticket holders and big Dayton fans. Nate saw that Dayton had lost their basketball game."

"As I approached Nate, ready to tell him the horrible story of the last 30 hours, Nate spoke first."

Mom, I have bad news for you. UD lost their game to Wisconsin.

"Reflecting later, Nate said my reaction was not what he expected. I did not seem to care about the basketball game. How could that be? Amanda approached. so I could tell them our story–the true bad news."

"I told them whatever I could remember about the story of the tide pools. After an abridged version, Nate's knees started to buckle, but he stood strong. I said something to Amanda about her mother being in the hospital from a terrible fall last Thanksgiving. She said, *Yeah, I'm done with Thanksgiving*. We got to the car and drove to the hospital."

"When Nate, Amanda and I walked in, Dean was no longer on BiPap machine and his blood/oxygen numbers remained great," Rose continued. "Despite the fact that this was only 24 hours since he first arrived in the hospital, he seemed so much like himself except for the cuts and scrapes everywhere. Nate and Amanda were probably expecting worse, but it's hard to relate how much Dean improved through the day on Wednesday."

"It is hard to imagine what their reaction was like compared to ours. We had been through so much. There was doubt about Dean living through the ordeal. Now he just looked like himself except he was in a hospital bed in a hospital gown."

Amanda, who is a doctor, told me later that I looked a lot better than she expected, given what she knew had happened and that I was in the ICU. From her experience, she knew how bad things could have been.

Soon thereafter, Stephen left again to pick up our son, Luke, who was coming in about 30 minutes later. All these things happened without any complaint from Stephen. He was taking care of things for his mom.

Luke was informed by Stephen of our ordeal as they came straight to the hospital. Now we had the whole family together. We had about 30 minutes before they had to leave ICU at 7:00 p.m. It was a great reunion.

Stephen asked Rose if we could invite rescuer Devron to dinner with our family that night. Rose told him of course to do so. He texted Devron, who said he was with his family. Stephen told him to bring them, we were all family now. Devron said he wasn't the only one. Could he invite Karl? Rose said, "Please, I'd love to see Karl."

Chapter 13: Normalcy & Improving, Wednesday PM

"Savor your existence; Live every Moment; Do not waste a breath"
Nando Parrado

Wednesday evening meant a new ICU nurse, Amber Wyse. Over the course of the evening, I was not the best patient, but she put up with me. Because I was feeling better, I wanted to do a lot more things. However, the catheter along with my true condition, as shown by my vital signs, were not going to allow that to happen. Because I felt so much better than 24 hours before, I thought I was healthy.

Like everyone else I worked with, Amber was patient and kind to me. With her, I got my first taste of food in a couple of days. I also got my own pitcher of iced tea to drink. It was a regular party now. It's funny to reflect on now, but when I met Amber eight months later in St. Croix, she remembered how important the pitcher of tea was to me. Sometimes the small things in life take on an outsized importance.

I did not sleep well that night for a number of reasons. Between one of the alarms going off, breathing treatments, emptying the bag tied to the catheter, and checking my vitals, it felt like I was up more than asleep. Now that my breathing was better and I was no longer cold, the aches and pains throughout my body were much more pronounced. Since I was cut up nearly everywhere on my body, I noticed that every small movement hurt someplace.

One of the toughest parts was the extreme cold in the ICU. Because they were in the process of building a new hospital, they were not investing in the infrastructure of the old one. Anyone who came into my room that night, technicians or nurses, was bundled up in layers of clothes. Amber told me most of them wore two pairs of pants to stay warm. I asked one of the nurses how cold it was. She told me it was 66 degrees in there.

I talked to Amber a little more, getting to know her and where she was from. I was rapidly becoming myself again.

* * * *

For the rest of the family, Wednesday night became one of the great memories of the trip. Stephen had been texting with Karl and Devron. At the same time, Courtney and Amanda were looking for a restaurant that would be open late enough to accommodate them. Only one of them was open until 10:00, so the family went there, Shupe's, an open-air, on-the-water restaurant. They got to meet the first two rescuers, Karl and Devron, plus Devron's family, in a much different setting and have dinner with them.

Karl's voice was hoarse from yelling down into the hole to me for so long. He told them that every time he heard those waves crash while I was in the hole, he made sure he yelled out because he did not want me to feel alone or abandoned. At one point, he looked at Nate and remarked that it was hard to do so because Nate looks a lot like me.

Rose reflected that it was hard to feel celebratory because we were still in the middle of everything. But having Devron and Karl there put the focus on all they did to give Dean a chance. He was kicking that chance's butt. Letting them know Dean was doing much better felt like the best news we could deliver to them.

While they were eating and enjoying everyone's company, Stephen suddenly pointed out two women walking by and asked, "Is that Dr. Bacon (my ER doc)?" Stephen got up from the table to walk after her. After the awkward, "Are you Dr. Bacon?" question, Stephen explained who he was and what was going on. He asked if Dr. Bacon and her friend would join in the family gathering. They joined the family at the table.

Rose was happy that she could update Dr. Bacon on my improved condition. It represented another opportunity to personally thank her for all her work and dedication. Rose knew that every chance to speak with the people who took care of me was a cherished moment.

Rose called that dinner *celebrating with a little bit of "I-hope-that-it-is-not-too-soon-to-celebrate"*. Having the others around allowed everyone to focus on the positives, instead of ruminating over what happened. It was a very good thing that the two rescuers, the doctor, and the whole family were there. It was a gift to all of us.

Courtney, who is the quiet one in the family, sat back and observed. For her, Stephen and Rose were "on point", being themselves for the first time since the incident. Stephen was up and about talking to everyone. He made everyone feel welcome and part of the family. Rose was trying to teach Devron's youngest son how to add 2+2=4. It was great for Courtney to see the two of them be themselves, even if it was only for a short while. It was a dinner that was semi-normal, family and friends sharing together, like vacation was supposed to be.

It wouldn't be this vacation if there was not one more little barrier to overcome.

After dinner, the family headed back to the house, exhausted from travel and the nature of the day. When they arrived at the house, there was no running water. One more small obstacle in a vacation filled with them. Rose's phone was gone to the bottom of the ocean, and that's where the number for our host was located. They wondered, "How are we ever going to get the water fixed?" Rose filled pots with water from the swimming pool so they could flush toilets. She was too exhausted to think about it more than that.

Luckily for the family, Amanda kept searching online until she was able to contact the host. The last obstacle of a very long day had been overcome. Exhausted and bewildered, everyone went to bed.

A maintenance worker came early Thursday morning and switched to the second cistern which gave them running water. All of them took a shower that morning, which was Thanksgiving.

Chapter 14: Disappointment, Thanksgiving 2022

"We must accept finite disappointment, but never lose infinite hope."
Martin Luther King, Jr.

It's Thanksgiving. A day of celebration. For our family, we remember Thanksgiving as a time to gather to eat too much and have fun playing board games. We look forward to time together. This year was going to be in a different place, but just as much fun. Until the incident happened. I still held out hope we could have a family gathering for Thanksgiving.

My morning began with more improvement overnight in my condition. I expected Steve to be my nurse again that morning. But the hospital was not very busy, so he was given the day off to enjoy. I was initially disappointed, but then I met Kristen Lee as my nurse. She was another great person to spend the next 12 hours with.

To be honest, she was not the person I wanted to spend the day with. I wanted to be at the house, with my family. I was focused on one thing - getting out of the hospital and being with my family on Thanksgiving.

Kristen allowed me to sit up in a chair for a while. This was the first time I had sat up since before the event. Another small step forward. She even took out the catheter on Thursday. Now I was allowed to stand up for the first time in nearly two days and walk to the bathroom. That may not sound like a big deal, but it was my Neil Armstrong moment ("That's one small step for a man, one giant leap for mankind"). Being able to walk, even a small distance, holding onto the bed, felt like such freedom. One more item on my progression.

Every one of the healthcare workers who came to see me was amazed at my progress. We talked about the improvement in "my numbers". I was gaining confidence that I would be getting out of the hospital and be able to spend Thanksgiving with my family.

One of the most enduring memories is when Dr. Lauren Bacon, my ED physician, came to visit me that morning. She had a lot to do with the improvement in my condition.

Dr. Bacon came up to see me in the ICU Thursday morning. It was very emotional for me to see her. She told me that she had two patients in ED on Tuesday night that were in bad shape, me being one of them. She told me that only one patient lived through the night, me. This helped me to begin to understand that my event was about way more than just me.

ED doctors like Dr. Bacon see lots of patients, in all kinds of condition, every day. It was important for her to see one of her patients doing much better. I was touched that I could be a good outcome for her. This conversation planted the seed that I needed to find and connect with everyone I could who helped me out.

The fact that she sought me out, in her busy day, was very meaningful to me. I was in no condition to get to know her on Tuesday night. I was fighting for my life, and was not me. Seeing her meant the world to me.

"I was off work on Wednesday. Your family told me how you were doing, but I wanted to see for myself," Dr. Bacon told me. "On Thursday, I was eager to find out what happened to you. Did you survive, had you gotten worse? I asked one of the nurses to take me to ICU. I had never been there."

"When I arrived, you were sitting up in bed, getting ready to eat. You looked so good. I think the one thing you wanted to do was get up and walk around. You were as surprised as we were how good you were doing. Despite the fact you were doing well, I knew you'd have a few more days in the hospital. I thought for sure I'd see you again on my Friday shift."

A pain specialist came to see me and assess my injuries. I had the impression they were going to be a reason I had to stay in the hospital longer than I thought I should have to. But after examining me and talking with me, she was quite positive about my status.

As I kept getting positive feedback, I started to think I was going to get out of the hospital. I would be able to spend Thanksgiving with my family. Talk about a great celebration!

But that was not going to happen.

Nurse Kristen bore the brunt of my complaining when I realized I was not going to get to spend Thanksgiving at home with my family. She was patient and listened to me. She advocated for me, to no avail. Unlike the others, she had to keep delivering me bad news ('you can't leave'); that was not a decision she got to make.

To be fair, I did not understand at the time how close I had been to death earlier. Nor did I understand how far I still had to go. While my breathing was much better, many of the rest of my systems were still recuperating. The chance of infection was still great. My electrolytes were still very messed up. A setback was possible. I did not realize that. I was focused on having Thanksgiving with my family.

Rose came back at the hospital at 10:00 a.m. by herself. The rest of the family was exhausted. They stayed back at the house to recover. Their holiday vacation was nothing like they had hoped for.

Rose had no idea the buzzsaw of frustration from me she was about to run into.

The ICU doctor had called in and talked to the nurses but was not showing up to check on me. From my perspective, I was better. I was allowed to eat and drink. I no longer had the BiPap machine or the tube. I felt so much better than I did 24 hours prior. No one told me I had any long-term issues. Why not let me go to have Thanksgiving with my family? Discharge me.

"Dean was very much himself except for his patience with his situation, Rose noted. "He wanted out. To be home with family."

"For the two of us at the hospital, Thanksgiving dragged. Dean was unhappy he was stuck there and was lobbying his nurse to be on Team Dean and get him discharged. I was disappointed for him. Not getting a direct answer as to why he had to stay was frustrating. We were acting in a vacuum of information. Our whole vacation was planned on having a fun Thanksgiving together and that was fading quickly."

She continued, "At that same time, I knew when he was discharged there would still be lots of care at home. So, while he was there, he was safe, and I was definitely okay with that."

Thanksgiving morning and afternoon dragged on. Rose and I were stuck where we did not want to be. Poor Kristen, our nurse, had no good news to deliver. I know I was unreasonably grouchy, but I just wanted to be with my whole family.

Stephen continued to be a wellspring of patience and support. He went out to get the family Thanksgiving dinner, bring it back to the house, and then bring the family to see me to at least say "Happy Thanksgiving". Unfortunately, due to a miscommunication, the whole food order was not complete. So, he had to hang out for 45 minutes in the grocery store waiting for mashed potatoes and green beans to be done. He brought those sides, along with the turkey, to the house and picked up everyone else. He never complained about having to be the chauffer and the errand runner. He was traumatized by the incident just like the rest of us, but he had duties to do. I was proud of him.

The rest of the family came to the hospital to see me around 5:00 p.m. They were warned I was not happy. The doctor had no intention of letting me go, but no one would officially tell me that. We talked for around for 45 minutes before the ICU closed. It was great to see them, but melancholy because I would be alone for Thanksgiving evening.

Back at the house, the family ate their Thanksgiving meal and then relaxed to watch movies. The meal was a mixed blessing of "not what we wanted to be doing" and "thankful that we were still going to have us all around". Rose was determined to accept the second item.

The meal was so normal that Rose doesn't remember much about it. But she does remember what happened afterwards. "We were watching movies from the 90's. Diehard 3 was on. There is a scene in the movie where the aqueduct tunnel dam is blown up and the tunnel floods with water. I could not watch. I had to leave the room. I couldn't breathe. The next movie was Princess Bride. When the Princess gets sucked down by the lightning sand in the fire swamp, I was again unable to breathe. Not sure when I'll be able to watch those scenes or enjoy those movies. Seeing someone trapped in a water-related danger was not a situation I could handle at the time."

Back at the hospital, I had my Thanksgiving dinner, alone. Not exactly what I had planned but I was fortunate to have a Thanksgiving dinner at all.

Michelle was my Thanksgiving night/Friday morning nurse. As Kristen introduced us, I asked Michelle if I could be candid with her. I told her how angry I was that I was not afforded the opportunity to go home on Thanksgiving with my family. She allowed me to blow off steam.

After hearing my story, she asked if my blood pressure and pulse rate were normally high. I told her, "No". Now she understood that the numbers that looked alarming to her as a nurse checking in on a patient for the first time were the result of other factors. My agitation made my condition look worse than it was. She understood where I was coming from.

The two of us settled into our routine. For me, it was the fitful sleep, the buzz of the machines, and my general uncomfortableness. Michelle would come in to check on me or respond to my requests for something to drink or to go to the bathroom.

We had a good talk over the evening, getting to know each other's backgrounds and learning how she became a nurse. With my strength returning, and the ability to stand up, I was much more myself.

But I was still unhappy that I missed Thanksgiving Dinner with my family.

Chapter 15: Release, Family Time, Return Home

"We have two lives, Roy: the life we learn with and the life we live with after that." Iris Gaines (Glenn Close) in the movie, The Natural

I woke up on Friday, November 25 and could hear my nurse Michelle talking with the doctor in a room nearby. I could not hear the full conversation, but it was clear she was advocating for my release. Occasionally, I could hear her mention one of my "numbers".

Around 8:00 a.m., the doctor came in to see me for the first time in two days. He checked my condition and talked through the situation. At one point, he told me, "I did not think you were going to make it out alive on Tuesday night". That is the first time I had a clearer indication of how bad my original situation was. I honestly did not know. I was in bad shape; I was so out of it mentally that I did not have a clue. My recovery on Wednesday was so fast and so sudden, I did not think I was ever very ill.

Then he told me I was going to be discharged. I was elated.

His instructions were pretty minimal. I had a few things I had to do. One was to take an antibiotic for a few days to make sure I did not get any further lung infections. Two was an inhaler for my respiratory system (I never took that one). Three was an Incentive Spirometer (the name is much more sophisticated than the product), a small lung exercise device. Exercise that will help me? I was all in on doing that.

Kristen was my nurse for the day again, so she had the "honors" of escorting me out of the hospital in a wheelchair. It was the first time I had seen the outside of the hospital and the first time I got to be outside in two and a half days.

It was also the first time I had worn clothes, other than a hospital gown, in almost three days.

Stephen and Rose were planning on heading out around 8:45 a.m. to go buy a new phone since her old one was somewhere at the bottom of the ocean. Then the hospital called on my behalf to tell them I was being discharged. For the first time since arriving in St. Croix, we had a positive change of plans.

Discharge happened very quickly. In the car in the hospital parking lot, Stephen took a selfie of the three of us. He sent it to John and Amie, the original people who called 911. They responded it was the best picture of their entire Caribbean vacation. We went straight home and got me settled. Stephen and Rose headed back out for a phone and lotion.

That afternoon, I napped and the rest of the family went to Buccaneer Beach. Stephen wanted to do something besides "death beach". They hung out for about an hour as a family and enjoyed the sun and water.

One of my first orders of business at the house was to take a shower for the first time in three days.

Although I am not an expert on romantic novels and movies, I think one of the staples in them is for the two romantic leads to take a shower together at some point in time. Huge glassed-in shower, romantic music in the background, the sounds of the ocean, etc. Well, Rose and I were about to take a shower together, but there was nothing romantic about it. I smelled terrible. My skin was cut almost everywhere. I could not move very much. Because of the stiffness of the healing scabs and my general stiffness from laying in a bed for a couple days, I could not reach most of my body. That is where Rose had a role to play. She was going to gently wash me and softly towel me off, because I could not do either.

It felt great to be clean and to smell clean. We were instructed to put Neosporin all over my body to keep infections away and Aquaphor to keep my skin moist. Rose smeared those two things all over me. The things you do for love. While my clothes stuck to my body, it felt good to have clothes on again. Between looking in the mirror, and having shorts and a short sleeve shirt on, I could see the extent of my cuts for the first time. It was not a pretty sight.

I rested much of that day. Later that day, Ben Torkelson, the third rescuer, and his son came by the house. We had his number thanks to

Stephen's diligence on the beach. This was the first time I got to meet Ben and see who he was. We shared our stories about what happened and the day's events. It was great to thank him and fill in blanks in his story.

That evening, Stephen and Nate brought take out home for dinner. Eating together with the family was a big deal. That was part of the reason for the vacation. It was fun to be back around the table and all of the noise.

The rest of our trip was time for relaxing and taking people back to the airport to return home. While we did not get to spend time doing what we originally planned to do, it was much better than any other alternative.

Saturday afternoon was spent with the first of a few calls to tell extended family members what happened to me. While we were not going to do a broadcast message of what happened, we felt it was important to tell family members we were closest to.

Both of my sisters are big Ohio State football fans. That Saturday was the Ohio State-Michigan football game, the biggest of the year for people who care about those things. We decided to wait until the game was over to call. Ohio State had lost, which is something Ohio State fans think should never happen. I remember both of my sisters telling me that after hearing my story, the Ohio State loss was not such a big deal. I guess I helped put things into perspective.

It was emotionally exhausting to retell the story. But it was a necessary part of my healing.

On Saturday night, two more of the rescuers, Devron and Jason (along with his family) came to visit me. Being able to tell his children that their father saved my life was a great thing to be able to do. I think children don't often know the result of their parent's work.

Karl and Malik came to visit me on Sunday. It was a warm reception to see their faces and (very gently) hug each other. We shared stories of the day. It was great for the family and I to interact with them. This meant that I had met the five main rescuers in person before I left St.

Croix. It is difficult to express how important and emotional this was for me. How do I properly thank someone for risking their own life to save mine? My emotions were very close to the surface.

On Sunday morning, all of our children were home or headed home. Rose and I were alone together. I was feeling strong enough for us to take a short walk in our neighborhood, similar to the one we had taken on our first morning in St. Croix.

Rose and I had return flights on Monday, November 28. I was still pretty weak. Rose had to drop me off at the airport and then return the rental car. As would become a new part of my life, I got the first "You are that guy?" reaction at the airport.

When we checked in at the TSA booth at the airport, we asked to get a pass to board the flight ahead of others because I was moving slowly and did not want to get bumped by others. I decided to explain to the TSA agent why I was making that request, because I otherwise looked perfectly healthy. When I mentioned the tide pools, she responded with "you are the guy? I read about you in the newspaper." I was even a minor celebrity in St. Croix now.

I think the fact that neither of us remember much about the flight and the drive home says that it was as normal as could be. Back to Ohio.

The next bad thing to occur was a rash I developed all over my body. I surmised it was a reaction to all of the medicine I was taking. We set up an appointment with my primary physician for the day after we returned (Tuesday). I needed to get this rash addressed immediately.

Chapter 16: Healing Body and Mind

"Everything can be taken from a man but one thing: to choose one's attitude in any given set of circumstances, to choose one's own way."
Viktor Frankl

When we returned to Dayton, I had an appointment with my primary care physician on Tuesday, November 29. As we walked in together, he told Rose and I, "Well, I know something is up because you're both here." We proceeded to tell him the St. Croix story.

His review of my condition was that I was doing well. He didn't see the need to do blood work, he felt like I did not have any long-standing issues. We had him look at my scrapes and the rash that had developed. He determined I was reacting to the antibiotic ointment and oral antibiotics. Since the wounds didn't appear infected, I stopped both.

He told me that he thought I would be "running by Christmas", less than one month away. I took that as a challenge to accept.

In about a week, the rash went away. Physically, I was doing well.

We both knew the next steps had to address our mental and emotional health. A near-death event takes a toll on your mental state. We were prepared to make sure that the mental and emotional injuries were looked after in a similar way to the physical injuries. Trauma has a way of burying itself inside the body, sometimes to protect us. This was going to be a longer, less straight-forward journey.

I wrote a blog post on November 30 that explained the whole incident and my miraculous rescue. Rose and I started telling more people about what happened. Word spread fast.

Also on November 30, Rose had her business networking meeting first thing in the morning. That was both a comfort and a challenge. She knew she had to tell the story about the incident to a group of 35 people who know her very well. The purpose of the meeting is not to tell personal stories, it is to network for each other's businesses. But this was a special circumstance.

"As I contemplated what to do, I felt like I was reliving the event that had only happened eight days ago," Rose relayed. "As I prepared to talk, I had to pause for breath. I told the story to the crowd. I received all the support I could ask for. I then took care of two of my (massage therapy) clients. It felt like a small return to normal life."

That night, Rose went without me to the improv comedy club where we perform. She got many hugs from people who had read my blog post. That Wednesday was a lot of support and a step forward in Rose's healing.

On December 13, I wrote a second blog post. This one was focused on my medical care. I wanted to make sure I honored all of the medical professional and tell my readers how great those folks were. Honoring others was part of my healing process.

Telling others my story and answering their questions was good therapy for me. It is amazing how emotional the first few times telling the story were for me. I could feel myself start to well up. I had to stop and gain my composure. The more I told it, the easier the story became to tell. Not because it was an easy story to tell. I could feel that talking about it was allowing that trauma hidden away to come out in the open. It was a signal to my mind and body that I did not need to hold onto anything.

"I could not tell the story without my breath catching because I felt thrown right back there," Rose told me. "I felt death was lurking right outside our door. Death felt like it had been cheated and was looking for the next opportunity. I became more risk averse than I ever was in my life. I noticed when someone is late or out of contact, my brain defaults to the thought that something bad has happened. That is not like me and is definitely something I want to heal. It is going to take a while."

We agreed that each of us would try some alternative therapy. We went separately to sessions with Doug Akerman of Meridian 180. Doug is one of the few certified Level 3 Energy Kinesiologists in the

United States. I won't even try to explain what Doug does. This is one thing from his web site: "Energy Kinesiology is an alternative health and wellness modality. It identifies, unravels, and clears energetic imbalances within a person. These energetic changes allow the body's own healing process to create changes at the physical level."

The sessions were non-traditional. After the first session, I could feel a difference in myself, a "lightening", as if a weight had been moved from my shoulders. It made a difference in my mental wellbeing.

Rose found that Doug helped her address some terror and fear she was sheltering. It opened up her to the very real emotions that had been set aside naturally in the hectic last few weeks.

* * * *

We have been married long enough that we know each other quite well. Both of us thought that the other was not dealing with the emotions. Rose had her concerns but did not express them out loud, trusting I was doing so "my way". At the same time, I didn't see Rose dealing with her emotions. I saw her working, a lot. I told her I thought she was throwing herself into work rather than taking care of herself.

"Mostly, I wanted to defend myself. Instead, I told Dean what other self-care things I was doing, just not with him." Rose reflected. "I promised I would ponder this because I wasn't seeing him doing things to heal emotionally. We decided the problem we weren't sharing the healing experiences we were having. We decided to share that journey more."

Having each other to share experiences with was a way to deal with the mental burdens. Rose and I have a different way of looking at most things. That diverse approach is a way to help each of us see outside our own viewpoints.

For example, I shared with Rose that people will hear this story and say, "it's a miracle". While I was okay with that, it felt like it didn't acknowledge what all those different individuals did for me to be alive and well.

Rose had an interesting perspective that helped open my mind.

"I get it. I think I've learned that miracles aren't the sky opening like in an old epic movie. Rather, miracles are made up of us," Rose summarized. "God puts in front of us something for us to do. When we say yes and do it, it's a small miracle. Sometimes when enough of those small miracles align or add up, we get the huge miraculous outcome that we got."

She went on, "I'll go back to the dragonflies and your mom. You said you got shoved by a third swell into the space, onto the ledge in the rock, where there was air. I can't help but believe that was your mom doing the shoving. That was a little miracle."

"Those tour guides showed up with their tour group, found an emergency, and jumped right in to help. Ben and his brother changed their original plan for the day and decided to head to the tidal pools instead. Thus, Ben, with the rope, was closer to us when the call came and he arrived 20 minutes before anyone else. Ben had the thought to throw his rescue rope in his vehicle. All these small miracles needed to happen for you to have a chance at surviving. And because these people said yes, I have more years with my husband."

This helped me put into context something I was wrestling with. It is okay to say miracles happened for me.

* * * *

A significant milestone for me was on the one-month anniversary of the event, December 22. I went out for a 3-mile jog, just like my doctor had said I would do. I was determined to get back to normal as best I could. It felt great to be out running again.

While running was great for me, it also opened up some areas needing consideration. One day, Rose and I were both at home. I left for a run and came back after 45 minutes. I've done that 100s of times since Rose and I have been married. But this one had shaken Rose. She told me that she was worried I was not home yet and had contemplated calling the neighbors to see if they saw me. Rose is not a worrier. I realized then how much the events in St. Croix had put her into "Mother Protector" role. This was a strong reminder that the event was very present for her, more than a month later. I needed to take care of myself and her.

I have had a lot of mind-body connections. In February, I noticed that I was not running as well as I would have liked. I could run the distances I wanted to. I was not hurting after a run. But I was running much slower than I should have been. I felt like I was exerting a lot of effort but not getting the results. Strangely, it felt like my feet were hitting the ground louder than normal. My performance was frustrating.

Rose recommended I go to another alternative therapy with Shelby, who is a muscle activation therapist. At my first appointment, Shelby diagnosed that my flight or fight mechanism was kicking in. Any person who has gone through trauma often has their most basic instincts and reflexes impacted. The subconscious brain cannot always distinguish between a run that is simply an exercise and one that is a traumatic situation depleting my resources. Given how important running is to my identity and well-being, it makes sense that my subconscious would use running as a warning signal.

Simply put, my body had taken the trauma of November 22 and deposited it into my most basic reflexes to protect me. Shelby had a protocol to "reprogram" my reflexes to not make an unconscious decision to fire every time. After a few appointments, I noticed an amazing difference. I was back to running comfortably. Another part of the emotional and mental turmoil had been identified and addressed.

Both Dr. Bacon and Amanda (the ED Respiratory Therapist) told me when I interviewed them later that they were certain they would see me over the weekend still in the hospital. Amanda said, "I thought it would Sunday or Monday until you got out of the hospital. You had taken so much salt water in and your body chemistry was all over the charts. It was trying to synchronize to homeostasis. I figured it would take that long to get you back. I was so surprised when I learned you checked out Friday morning. Amazing."

* * * *

"The Return" became a big part of the mental journey. In February 2023, I had an idea; I wanted to return to St. Croix. I had two important reasons for wanting to go back.

First, it was important for my further mental development to face my fears. Would I be scared of the ocean? I needed to get back into water, sooner rather than later, to prove that it was not a dangerous spot most of the time. I also wanted to rewrite the narrative of St. Croix. It needed to be much more than "the place I nearly died". I wanted to turn the narrative a little. St. Croix is an island paradise with a lot of great people. I needed some time to make that new connection.

The second reason is a trip would provide an opportunity to meet more of the people involved in saving my life. Rose and I could jointly thank them and also interview them for this book. There many people that I had never met. The helicopter crew and most everyone in the ER, for example, hardly saw me conscious. They got to see me at my worst. I wanted them to see me healthy. The real Dean. I also wanted to see them for who they are, because I didn't get to do so in November.

When I first said it, Rose thought I was joking (which I am known to do). When she realized I was serious, she had some trepidation. When I told her I wanted to go back to the tide pools to see them and to get pictures, I remember her asking, "Can't we just hire a photographer to do that for us?"

Rose had a visceral reaction when I brought up the idea for us to return to St. Croix. She said, "My stomach knotted. I took a deep, slow breath and asked why and what he wanted to accomplish. When he gave me his reasons, I saw it was important to him. He didn't want to be afraid of the water. He wanted to face that fear. I told him he was not allowed to get back into that tidal pool. He assured me he would not."

Rose being Rose, she was all in once she saw how important it was to me.

We started our trip with a visit to Puerto Rico, where the 911 Command Center and helicopter crew are located. On a side trip, we drove to a nearby beach to spend a little time in the Caribbean Sea. There was a steep grade to the beach at the water's edge. Thus, the wave and the undertow were churning a bit there and it sounded powerful. Just getting close to that water made my stomach tighten. Once we each got in the water and enjoyed the surf, all was well. After a while I told Rose, "I guess I need to put my head underwater and see how that feels." I did it and it felt okay so we stayed in for 15 minutes. We considered it a success and step one to not being afraid of the ocean.

This trip was originally termed a "vacation". After contemplation, I came to recognize it actually was a "book research" trip. After having experienced it, Rose came up with the right description, a "pilgrimage".

* * * *

Both of us have found great joy and healing in telling our story. We've told it so many times, to so many people, but it never gets old. It connects us with others. It offers us a chance to be real.

Our world is now divided into two groups. One group contains those people who have heard or read about what happened to me. The other group is those who have not. It is immediately clear where someone sits in that duality. Rose and I have laughed together when we talk to someone and St. Croix never comes up. Afterwards, Rose smiles and says to me, "They don't know what happened, do they?"

There have been a few cases where someone who did not know me heard the story and would say to me, "You're the guy I heard about!". They might have read or heard some part of the story, but did not know me. Now I put a face to a story they knew about. It is fun to see their reaction.

* * * *

I realized that I needed to make a concerted effort to honor and thank everyone. Thus began a many months-long effort of gathering information on those who took care of me during the rescue and afterwards.

I reached out to the US Coast Guard and the hospital to gather information. At the same time, I was finishing my first book, *Doable Change: Making Incremental, Achievable Difference in Your Career and Life*. I needed to get it done so I could start writing more about this new experience. I scaled down my paid work hours in order to attend to these things and get stronger.

Writing is a way for me to get my thoughts and emotions out. It is therapeutic for me. Besides the two blog posts, I started writing down things I remembered from those days as a precursor to this book. Trying to get the names of people who saved me was work that helped my mental state. Each small effort was a step forward for me.

* * * *

It was important for us to realize that while we had each other, our son Stephen was on his own. More than any other person on earth, he shared the story. He had the added burdens of nearly dying himself and sharing the downs and ups of that afternoon with Rose. We checked in with him regularly, knowing how hard our journey was.

Stephen shared this touching story from his experience. "It is near Christmastime (2022) and I am slowly getting back into a rhythm of life. Brad, an acquaintance from my golf club, was sitting next to me at dinner, so I told him the story of St. Croix. Brad has two small children and owns his own business. "

"Later I got a text from Brad, *I am appreciative of you sharing your story. I am thankful you and your dad are doing well. It reminds me of how thankful I should be. I appreciate the reminder of how lucky we all are and makes me thankful for so much in my life.*

"*I appreciate these stories because I love being connected to people. Your story connects us in a way and how appreciative and thankful we should be to each other. It touched me in a way that I shared it at our employee Christmas party today with all of my employees because we should realize how much we can impact each other's lives."*

Brad's story is a great reminder that we never can know the impact we have on others when we are open and honest. It helped me understand that part of the meaning of my incident is a nudge to be more engaged with others. As Rose has said, "God puts in front of us something for us to do. We get the choice whether to respond with a *yes* or a *no*.

* * * *

On Friday, June 9, 2023 we did the only "vacation" thing on our visit to Puerto Rico and St. Croix. We went to witness sunrise over the Caribbean Sea at Point Udall (the farthest east spot in the US to see a sunrise). Sunrises hold a special meaning for Rose. We intended to watch the sunrise in November 2022 with the family, but none of us were up for it then.

As the sun slowly began to emerge over the horizon on that day, we were both silent and moved by the enormity of the view. Witnessing the sunrise together was more valuable than we could have expected. That morning together was soul nurturing and quietly life affirming.

It felt like it created a bookend to our St. Croix trips. The first had started in complete darkness and this one saw the rising of a new light.

We know our journey is still ongoing; this day felt like we turned one more meaningful chapter in our journey for meaning.

Dean with Karl Frederick, upon return in June 2023. Karl is the first person to make verbal contact when I was down in the cavern.

Ben Torkelson (L), Dean, and Devron Smith (R). Ben's decision to put his rescue rope into his jeep the day of the rescue was one of the keys to survival. Devron (holding a thank you rock we gave each of them) made the decision to change from tour guide to rescuer.

Malik Garvey. Malik was the ambulance driver and EMT. I am wearing the rescue shirt he gave me off of his back that fateful day.

Jason Henry, Rescue St. Croix volunteer. One of the six on the rocks with me.

The US Coast Guard helicopter crew, (l to r). Beau James, Curren Hinote, Billy Boardman, and Travis Cox. These four pulled off an extraordinary mission in tough conditions.

Rose and Dean with Cadira, our ED nurse

Kristen, ICU nurse Thursday and Friday

Amber Wyse, Wednesday night ICU nurse

Steve Chumra, Wednesday a.m. ICU nurse.

This is the hole I was sucked down. It is about 2.5 feet by 1.5 feet, slightly larger than the size of a carryon bag you may take on an airplane.

This picture was taken in June 2023. In November 22, when the incident in the hole happened, this was covered with a couple feet on raging water.

The view out to the tide pools from the beach. Rose and Stephen sat here waiting. You can't see the 2nd tide pool from this vantage point.

Tide pool #1 looking back towards the beach. The ocean is to the left of the rocks on the left of the picture. The cliff on the right side of the picture was of particular concern for the helicopter crew.

Gov. Juan F. Luis Hospital and Medical Center in St. Croix, US Virgin Islands, the place where I was brough back to health.

Be a donor to a worthy cause:

Gov. Juan F. Luis Hospital and Medical Center

www.TheLedgeBook.com

Click on the "Donate" Button

All donations will go towards the support of the hospital. We have set up the RosaDean Foundation Fund #5112 as a component fund of The Dayton Foundation.

THE
SEARCH
FOR
MEANING

Chapter 17: The Quest.

"However this may be, there is no way in which I can have another man put where I am. I am here. I must do the best I can, and bear the responsibility of taking the course which I feel I ought to take."
Abraham Lincoln

As I worked my way back to normal life, I knew two things. One, my life had changed forever. Two, I needed to explore the meaning of these events more deeply. I looked forward to the challenges ahead. My mindset was this: I need to find new meaning out of the event and its aftermath. There had to be something that follows a life-defining situation, more than just carrying on with the rest of my life.

I am fortunate in a lot of ways. My life was saved. I have no deep, life-altering physical or mental challenges. I am at an age in my life where I have time and space to be more self-reflective.

My circumstances are unique to me. Sharing my journey and what conclusions I have come to might serve as an inspiration and challenge. If there is one lesson from November 22, 2022, it is that life can be very fleeting. Don't wait until "someday" or "when I have time" to think about your life and its purpose. I almost did not have the chance to do that.

First up is my learning from this experience needs to be meaningful to the lives of some cohort larger than me and the members of my family. After all, I was saved, shouldn't there be some higher meaning to my life to share with others? I had been awarded a gift; the gift of more time spent on this earth. Most of us don't go through an event believing your life is over, only to have it given back to you. I can only speak for myself. It is humbling. More importantly, it is invigorating.

I had a number of questions that I needed to answer. Among them were these big three:

- Why did this happen to me?
- Why did I survive?
- What am I supposed to do about it?

What follows is my viewpoint of what it is like from the inside. What was the journey like to gain some understanding, to gather some answers? How did I approach listening and learning? What were some of the answers I found? I recognize that anyone else's journey in life and mine are not the same. Perhaps in being honest about my journey, you will discover something.

Like so much of life, my thinking took a lot of twists and turns. What I originally believed to be true often was modified as time, knowledge, and reflection occurred. I was reminded, again-and-again, that life is a mystery. What we think is probably the truth when we initially consider it is not necessarily the only truth. I don't hold the answers. I get to choose what I want to be the final answer—for me.

Many of us have deep beliefs. I can assure you that if you talk to enough people, you will find people with beliefs about the meaning of life that are very different from your own. Consider me to be in that category. It is not that I am right or not. I simply am at this spot at this moment in my life. Just like the metamorphosis from adolescence to teenager to young adult, for example, changes what is important and meaningful to us, so it is with this journey.

Chapter 18: Why, Why, Why?

"There is a thin, elusive line between acceptance and surrender." Isaac Lidsky.

Why did this event happen to me?

Why did I survive?

Those two questions have dominated my thinking since that day. I can't ignore that I nearly died. It was all so sudden and unexpected. I was miraculously rescued. What is behind those series of events? Why was my destiny on that day different from all of the other people who die, unexpectedly and tragically?

Many people have shared their viewpoints on these questions. Most fall into one of two perspectives:

God has a plan for you

A string of lucky, haphazard events came together

After coming home, my reaction to both of those perspectives was one of discomfort, for two major reasons.

Reason #1 is that both perspectives simplify a complex series of moments.

Simplifying the unknown or mysterious is how we are all wired. It is a natural part of the way we make sense of the world. If we don't have an answer, we use our experiences and knowledge to come up with the most plausible answer (to us). Often, "not knowing" is a worse outcome that "knowing". Finding a simple answer makes the world a little less mysterious.

For example, if our team loses the game, we try to assign blame (inadequate coach, the officials cheated, this player is no good). If we get laid off from a job, maybe it's due to our lousy boss. When a celebrity dies, we want to know the cause of their death. Why does that actually matter? We don't really know the celebrity. I think it is because we want the story to have a clear ending.

In her book, *Genealogy of a Murder*, author Lisa Belkin explains how we often draw conclusions later in time, once we know more of the story. With a known outcome, we can plausibly draw a line from one act to another. She writes, "History divides neatly into chapters only in retrospect. In real time we experience it as a jumble, a hurtling through the darkness by the light of an inadequate lamp."

In the immediate aftermath of an event, its causes and impact are not clear. Only after we have time and space to render judgment do we put the pieces together and build a story. The explanation we come up with later allows us to keep the (relatively) orderly story we have imagined in our minds.

I understand the urge for answers and the need for simplicity. I just did not feel comfortable with it initially.

Reason #2 is that I did not want to be the center of the story. I felt the efforts of others (rescuers, helicopter crew, health care workers) were being diminished when the spotlight was on me.

If God chose me to be tested and then He saved me, or to be told "Your Guardian Angel was watching over you" sounded to me like God and I are all that matter. If I hear "random chaos" is the answer, the actions of so many brave and talented people are inconsequential. I believe they deserve more credit than to chalk it all up to "things happen".

While I am sure Karl, Devron, and Ben could not exactly explain why they took the action they did, that does not mean it was haphazard. Their character and experiences drove them to make fateful decisions.

The skills of the helicopter crew and the health care workers were built over a long time. Why those particular individuals were in St. Croix and Puerto Rico on that particular day is luck. But their actions were made deliberately and expertly. In my mind, talking about Dean's bravery or luck missed out on the opportunity to talk about the excellence of others.

If the spotlight is on me, we are diminishing all of their contributions. That did not feel right to me. If I am being honest, my deflection of my role was a defense mechanism. Time helped me understand that reality.

Making More Sense of the Divine Intervention Viewpoint

One day in church we had a reading from the Old Testament. In it, Samuel was sleeping and heard a voice calling out to him. He went to Eli to ask him what he wanted. Eli said he did not call Samuel and instructed him to go back to sleep. This happened a couple times before Eli realized Samuel was being called by God. Eli told Samuel to respond to the voice by saying he was listening.

For the divine interventionists, this is a clear case that Samuel was selected by God. We don't need to know why. We know He did.

We can read of more people who God selects (Moses, Mary, Abraham, etc.). It feels like a small number get called. But maybe it is not. Perhaps many are called but only some of them act on it. For every Samuel, there may be more than one unknown person, a "Louie" or a "Susie" who was spoken to by God. Maybe they did not hear the call. Perhaps they had no one to help them interpret the voice. it could be that they did not have the capacity to act on the message. It might be their story never got written down. Or their impact was relatively smaller.

The "club" of those spoken to by God is limited by the written record. Maybe reality is different. That helps me understand that I am not necessarily a member of a select few, but a member of a larger group.

Where does Eli fit in the story? He was there to help Samuel understand. Often, we need someone at our side to guide us. Samuel had that person.

With this perspective change, I could make sense that the people telling me "God has more work for you" are not trying to burden me. They are helping me hear the call, like Eli did for Samuel.

Being saved does not mean I am special or I am better than those who do not get saved. It is simply the reality of the situation. I don't need to reject people saying "The Lord decided it was not time for you to go." I need to recognize that their perspective makes sense.

Understanding the "Things Happen" Viewpoint Better

"Things Happen" thinking begins with the idea that God does not have a master plan for all of us nor is He executing on that plan. God does not have a specific "it's your time" for any of us. He is not watching over every action and making a decision whether someone lives or not.

We build our life through choices, not by acting out a script God has already planned. Moments are presented to us (perhaps by God) and we get to choose how we act. The consequences of our choices, and the choices of others around us, lead to our life. New, unpredictable moments come as a consequence of those choices. Our life is like a decision tree, branching in numerous directions at key points in time.

My friend Phil had another spin on this idea when he wrote to me about my event, "I have always believed in a random chaos theory. God created a world where all things are possible and occur in many combinations and permutations. God created the ocean and all of its elements. That wave may crash on those rocks hundreds of times a year and anyone standing there will be impacted. If no one is there it is a non-event. In a similar vein, if it happened on another day to another person there may not have been the right people to help in time."

The author Brian Klaas writes in his book, *Fluke: Chance, Chaos and Why Everything We Do Matters*, "Many of these (unexpected) events were triggered by flukes: small, chance happenings that were arbitrary, even random, and could easily have turned out otherwise."

Once I really thought about this "Things Happen" perspective, I realized it is not saying "all events are random". If it did, I have no control and my choices do not make a difference. It is simply saying life is not something we can completely control, but we still get to make choices and discover the outcome.

Understanding this, I recognize that by looking forward, and trying to make good choices, is a better use of my time than trying to make sense of what happened. I need to move ahead, taking advantage of the power that the series of moments (mine, the rescuers, and the healthcare professionals) gave to me.

My Learning

I had a nephew who died years ago, suddenly and tragically, at a very young age. I remember the priest speaking at the funeral, anticipating what we were all thinking. He said, *we are not supposed to know the answer to these kinds of questions (why did my nephew die at a so young age) here in this life. We'll find the answer when we meet God.* That struck me as comforting. His words allowed me to understand that I am not supposed to have the answer. It will be revealed to me at the time I meet God.

I've applied that same thinking to my current situation. Trying to definitively explain why I lived is unknowable in this life. It is a mystery not to be understood.

As Timothy Keller writes in *Making Sense of God*, "Ancient people did not assume that the human mind had enough wisdom to sit in judgment on how an infinite God was disposing of things. If you believe in an infinite God, how reasonable is it to assume a finite human mind should be able to evaluate His motives and plans?"

That thinking connects with my logical mind. There is no way to know what God's plan is for in this world. I am humble enough to say that I do not know His plan or His reasons for doing things.

I've learned so much about myself and how we all rationalize the unknowable. Trying to find definitive answers where life and death are involved is frustrating. The answer to the "Why me" question is unknowable. Using my energy to justify an answer is counter-productive. I have been wasting my time trying to explain and answer every "why" question I had about this event. I simply need to make a choice to recognize this happened. I was spared. Now I have the choice to do something about it. Every moment spent rejecting other's perspectives or trying to justify my thoughts is a moment not spent doing good.

It does not matter what story (Divine Intervention or Things Happen) best resonates with any of us. What matters is the choice we make to move forward in life.

That is the best I can do for my peace of mind.

Rose's Perspective

Rose often says she feels like it is her responsibility to "listen to what God is saying to me". That is an interesting way of thinking about our moments of obligations and opportunities. Sometimes the message is clear. Often it can be interpreted in different ways ('maybe God thinks it is okay for me to have that chocolate ice cream tonight').

"This says to me that God is not going to force you to do anything. He loves you and is trying to help you understand the right path. You get the choice to listen. None of us are perfect, so we won't make the right choice every time. But if we consciously choose to listen, we have a great start."

"This whole event has deepened my faith. I'll stand by the thought that miracles are made up of us doing whatever God puts in front of us that needs to be done in the moment. They are all little miracles when I notice things God has given me to do and I go do them. I trust that God is doing the same with many others and that others are going to do the same. I've always believed that people are mostly good if you give them the chance to be."

She has a newly-renewed humble gratitude that touches everything in her day. That includes being grateful for running water and other very basic conveniences that she took for granted before. A realization about how lucky she is that the grocery store shelves are full. And no matter the price, gasoline is plentiful and there to purchase when she needs it. She sums up her feelings, "I'm grateful to be alive. I'm grateful for the people in my life who I get to love through laughter and tears. I was given this life to love God by loving others. I am grateful for every day I get to do that."

Chapter 19: So Many Questions, So Many (un)Certainties

You need to be so careful when there is one simple diagnosis that instantly pops into your mind that beautifully explains everything at once. That's when you need to stop and check your thinking." Donald Redelmeier

Telling the story many times, I have been asked a lot of questions. Each of those causes me to look inside and try to recall. While the answer may be clear, the "why" is often not. I've learned that what I was certain about often has a lot of holes in it. Digging deeper has helped me understand that so much is unknown and subject to interpretation.

One question that many people asked me prompted much reflection: "What were you thinking about when you were in the cavern?"

The more I got asked that question, the more I found myself digging deeper into what I was thinking and why.

Amanda Ripley, in her book *The Unthinkable: Who Survives When Disaster Strikes and Why,* writes about the various reactions that individuals have to disasters. Her own interviews and research found different reactions. One very common reaction is panic, a sudden uncontrollable fear or anxiety, often causing wildly unthinking behavior. Another potential reaction is paralysis. Think of an animal that is startled. Often the animal will "freeze" as a defense mechanism. A third reaction is a type of paralysis reaction characterized as "negative panic". Ripley writes, "Paralysis seems to happen on the steepest slope of the survival arc, when almost all hope is lost, when escape seems impossible, and when the situation is unfamiliar to the extreme."

That last sentence described my situation accurately. When I read that passage, I recognized I probably exhibited negative panic. I did not act rashly. I did not act unthinkingly. While staying in the same spot held a near-certainty of death, no valid option appeared to make me change my thinking. My subconscious reaction ended up being the right one.

Later in her book, Ripley writes of Clay Violand, a survivor of the 2007 Virginia Tech mass shooting: "Human beings think, reflect, and make decisions. We don't always realize how much other work our brains are doing all the time, with or without us. In retrospect, Violand had created a narrative, as all survivors do, about what he did." She writes: "at the time, he adds, he didn't feel like he was making choices at all. Only now that I think about it a month later, I guess I had a strategy."

That is the best I can do to describe what I did. I did not know at the time that I had a plan. Reflecting on it now, I had a strategy that ended up being the right one. My situation was hopeless. I was trapped in an underwater cavern for more than 40 minutes with no escape route and no one knowing I was still alive. Yet somehow, I did not give up hope, consciously or subconsciously.

Ripley's book began opening up new venues for me. I understood the power of our brain to make decisions based on our experiences. In the cavern, I had no specific conscious thoughts, but my brain was working on the one decision that was the best for me.

* * * *

The idea of being closed off in a small, dark space is something that a lot of people wondered about.

"I could not have survived because I am claustrophobic," is something I have had heard from many people. It is a common reaction. It makes a lot of sense. The idea of darkness and small spaces is scary. Add rising water and an unknown location, and a scary picture comes to the fore. Many of us have experienced some level of claustrophobia in far less dangerous situations than the one I was in. I've heard, "It would have creeped me out" a lot of times.

I don't remember ever being claustrophobic during the time in the hole. I believe it had something to do with the circumstances. When your life is truly on the line, your focus and vision sharpen.

The reality of the situation was clear. I was trapped in this very tight, dark spot with water coming in on me. I was going to die. I had to be ready for the next wave to come in and slam me into the rocks. My attention was pretty focused. I did not have time to worry about the space itself closing in on me.

* * * *

"Your Guardian Angel must have been watching over you," is another statement I encountered a lot. It is a natural reaction. Many religious faiths believe in them. It is a staple of movies and books. The idea that someone (something?) is watching over us is a source of comfort. In a similar way, some people wanted to know if I heard any voices from God or angels. To be honest, I do not remember any voices until I heard Karl's voice. In my mind, I could call that a heavenly voice.

I think about this way: I don't know what an angel sounds like. I know that my spouse, family, and friends love me. They did not have to be present for me to feel their love. Perhaps that is the way angels (whether the guardian type or not) communicate. Through love. Some greater force kept me going when there was no hope as the time passed and no one knew I was under the rocks in the water.

The interesting thing is we all get to call my survival reaction whatever we want. Courage. Strength. Guardian Angel. Some higher power that wanted me to stay around for a longer time for some purpose. Maybe it is a combination of those things. We each get to choose which name we wish to give it. Whatever it is, it is part of life's mystery.

* * * *

"Do you have any nightmares about the incident?". My situation in the hole has the makings of a nightmare. Almost everyone has a fear of drowning. My drowning was going to be particularly long. I was conscious for a long time. The water was slowly drowning me. People say to me that they think they would have nightmares all the time. I get that.

I have not had one nightmare or flashback. There is probably a combination of reasons why I have not. I did therapy. I addressed the issue before it could bury itself inside me. Writing about it almost immediately afterwards probably helped.

Being open about what happened is a difference for me. Might that keep the nightmares at bay? I am much more willing to ask people if they know my story or bring it up with strangers than I might normally do with information about me. I am a private person by nature and am not one who likes to be the center of attention. This new-found openness is a good thing. I've told the story hundreds of times, but never get tired of talking about it. I figure that exposing it keeps it from "hiding" in my subconscious.

* * * *

Sometimes ideas popped into my conscious through reading. For example, a concept resonated with me sprung from a few pages in the middle of a book I was reading. Those pages on post traumatic growth helped me understand that my brain was going to provide me with a chance for evolution. I instantly became aware of that opportunity.

Richard Tedeschi and Lawrence Calhoun are experts on post traumatic growth, the idea that surviving a trauma leads to an "adaptive spiral of positive development which leads to an awaking of a new self". I had the opportunity to utilize my trauma to awake a new self. Perhaps the event was a way presented to me to try to grow. That is one way to understand "why" this happened – for my own development, if I chose to explore it.

In the book *How Minds Change*, the author David McRaney writes: "in the frightening and confusing aftermath of trauma, where fundamental (self) assumptions are severely challenged, people must update their understanding of the world and their place in it. If they don't, the brain goes into panic, unable to make sense of reality."

"People must update their understanding of the world and their place in it". I feel like that sentence is so true with me. While I do not want to exaggerate the change in me and profess that I am a totally changed man, I am different now. I was very self-reflective before. I am more so now. I have a new appreciation for where I spend my energy and my brain power. Recognizing that those are finite resources, and I don't know how long I might be on this earth, I utilize them more preciously.

I don't feel pressure that I must have a more profound place in this world. I am not supposed to be a superhero or a prophet for others. I am just supposed to be a more aware version of me.

McRaney continues: "(people) shed a slew of outdated assumptions that, until the trauma, they never had to question, and thus never knew were wrong. People report that it feels like unexplored spaces inside their minds have opened up, ready to be filled with new knowledge derived from new experiences."

I feel like my mind has been opened up. I try to lean into that opening up and be willing to explore. The best I can describe it is that some small percentage of my unconscious brain has been transformed to conscious thought. I just need to take the time and utilize it.

McRaney continues this thought, "To move forward, to regain a sense of control and certainty, you realize some of your knowledge, beliefs, and attitudes must change, but you aren't sure which. What is clear, however, is there is no option to continue as if your current models are true, so you enter into a state of active learning in which you immediately and constantly consider other perspectives, honestly assess your weaknesses, and work to change your behaviors to resolve the crisis. The process is automatic. No one chooses to seek meaning after trauma or to grow a new self in its aftermath. It's a biological switch, a survival mechanism that comes in line when needed."

A person working through trauma is following a natural path that is part of our way of thinking according to McRaney. Rose might call this "listening to God and acting on it". After all, who created the "biological switch"? Many would say God.

Why were these few pages in that particular book I was reading presented to me? I do not know. Obviously, I was receptive to them. They helped make me aware as to why I am thinking some of the things I am now, which I may not have thought consciously before.

The words in the book serve as a reminder that I am going through a process. I needed a great reminder that we are all presented with moments for decisions all the time. It is up to us to stop, recognize them, and decide to do something about them.

It is also important for me to say I am not comparing myself to people who have had even more life altering trauma such as sexual assault, horrific accidents, serious illness, or suffered combat injuries. There are different kinds of trauma. Compared to most people, I suffered very little. But it is critical to my mental health that I acknowledge that I did suffer trauma and to deal with it. From what I have read, our brains are not great at distinguishing those difference in traumas. Otherwise, as McRaney writes, I could consign my brain to go into panic.

* * * *

This mix of what others have asked me and said to me, what I read, and how I react to each is an alchemy for what I am to become.

Just because someone feels strongly that what they believe is true does not mean they are imposing their will on me. I don't need to disregard their feelings. Nor do I need to defend my viewpoint. Recognizing this is how we make our way through life; I am the beneficiary of many viewpoints. Why not learn from them?

To search for simplicity and answers in a world that is neither simple or easy to answer is how we operate by default. It is not bad. But by simplifying we miss out on the richness of the mystery. In a way, November 22, 2022 presented me with a look behind the curtain.

Perhaps that is part of the message my Guardian Angel was presenting to me.

Chapter 20: What Are We Supposed To Do About It?

"We do not receive wisdom, we must discover it for ourselves, after a journey through the wilderness which no one else can make for us, which no one can spare us; for our wisdom is the point of view from which we come at last to regard the world." Marcel Proust

I tell everyone that 11/22/22 is an inflection point in my life. I look at my life with a very distinct "before" and "after" November 22.

What am I supposed to do about this "after" life on earth? The option of going back to my daily life and acting as if the events of November 22 were simply another step in my life was a possibility. I am a private person by nature. I have a good life, why not go back to that?

I rejected that thinking. I can't go back to "pre–November 22 Dean".

On the other extreme, I could become a completely changed man. My life could have new meaning and new purpose. I could be a witness to the miraculous, unknown power that watches over our lives.

I rejected that approach also. I joked with some that I was not going to be a person standing on a prominent street corner with a sign saying, "Repent because the End is Near."

One day I was working on a blog post. The gist of the blog post was pondering about how we present ourselves to the outside world. The catalyst for this post was the abuse and trolling (he called it terrorizing) a father who had lost his 6-year-old son to a sudden, tragic death was receiving from strangers. His crime? He supported vaccinations. What kind of person sends a note that says, "Congratulations, you killed your son" to a grieving father?

That passage had me thinking about how I present myself to the world. While I don't think I do anything near that egregious, I have my faults.

Later that same day, I was out running errands. I chose a "short cut" to avoid the traffic. But The Universe (or God or The Game) had other ideas. A car was placed in front of me that was determined to drive the 25 mile-an-hour speed limit. As I found myself getting closer-and-closer to that car, it struck me. This was a test of my intentions.

I started laughing to myself and slowed to a near stop. I had been writing in that blog post about trying to be a better person, not an obnoxious one, and I got an immediate test. If I start to notice the tests placed in front of me, maybe I can make a better impact on the world. We all know we get tested; we probably miss 99% of those moments. Maybe I can do better than that.

There are the few concrete things I am actively working on to answer the question, "What are you going to do about this event?"

#1 The Hug

Ask me the most important change I have made in my life, and the answer is easy. It is The Hug.

Rose and I are definitely closer since the event. If you asked most people, it would be hard to believe we could be any closer. But now, life has been irreparably changed.

Some mornings, if we both happen to wake up at the same time, we will take a few minutes to hug in bed. Rose will often say something like "for five minutes" because she knows I am not the kind of person to lounge around in bed. In the past, one or the other would have woken up, looked to see if the other is awake and if not, gotten up to start the day. That's changed.

The author Gretchen Rubin noted, "The days are long but the years are short." That was all the impetus I needed to do a little thinking.

The Hug is an example of cherishing one of life's events in a meaningful, complete way. It is simple, yet profound.

What is The Hug? Rose and I make sure we have a meaningful hug every day of the year. Not a short, "I am thinking about other things I need to do" hug. Not a passing, "shoulders touching but not actually connecting" hug. Nope. To meet the goal, it needs to be a real, "I love you and acknowledge that you mean a lot to me" hug. It has to last at least ten seconds long. our focus needs to be in one place – hugging the other. I can feel her body breathing and relaxing as we hug. A strong, lasting connection, every time.

I told Rose this was one of my goals for 2023 and beyond. Since we both know that, The Hug happens daily. We look forward to doing The Hug. It does not happen at the same time of the day. Nor does it happen in the same place. But it happens. For those ten seconds, life stops and we are together. That is reframing a moment that normally happened into something more meaningful.

Rose and I have been married since 1983. Making a small moment more purposeful only makes our relationship better.

For Rose, The Hug has a different, but important origin story. When I got out of the hospital, my skin had a lot of healing to do. More than 75 percent of my body was covered with scrapes and wounds. She helped bathe me and dress my skin with antibiotic cream and a lotion. After I contracted a rash from that treatment, my skin was so uncomfortable.

"So, here it was a week after the incident and I still could barely touch Dean", Rose reflected how frustrating this was to her. "Of the two of us, I am the more likely to need a hug. Touch has always been important to me. That's why I became a massage therapist. I understood the value of touch in connecting, healing, and quality of life."

She remembers the day, December 10, when I walked into the kitchen and said, "My skin feels better. I'm not itching anymore. I feel pretty normal." She immediately asked, "Does this mean I can hug you?" We hugged and it felt so good to do that normal thing. From her perspective, even if I hadn't noticed that we hadn't been hugging, she was very aware of it, in an almost visceral way.

"A couple weeks later on a walk with our daughter, Dean was sharing his goals for the new year," she continued. "Number one was to hug me every day. I was immediately thinking of that scene in the kitchen. In that moment I thought Dean understood how meaningful that hug is to us and he wanted it, too. Him making it a priority is a wonderful gift to me and us. I'm all in."

#2 Connect, more often, with purpose.

It is easy for me to go a few days without connecting with anyone. I work from home. I go on my runs alone. As an introvert, I am comfortable with solitude and quiet. Give me a great time to run, a beautiful place to hike, or an interesting book to read, and I will be content. I generally do not like crowds and noise.

Since November 22, I am much more aware of the value in connecting with others. It may be for my own wellbeing. It may be for others. It is well documented that we are all suffering from an epidemic of loneliness. Perhaps I can change that with a call, getting together for a drink, or a written acknowledgement. My attention may be the thing someone else needs that day.

There might be something I can do for a friend, acquaintance, or someone I just got to know. Staying connected makes sure I keep that opportunity alive. I've read enough to know that having better relationships is a key to a healthy, happy life.

I am not doing this only for me. I am doing it for someone else. I don't know what kind of day, week, month, or year a person is having. Making a connection just might change their feelings. It feels right to take an attitude that I ask a little more of myself in order to help someone else.

As Timothy Keller writes in *Making Sense of God*, "If we are going to live rationally and use our minds well, we need new hearts. We need something that draws us out of our desperate search for self-fulfillment, affirmation, and value and makes us capable of loving other beings, not for our sake but for theirs."

I'm good at taking care of myself. Can I be equally as good at taking care of others?

#3 Enhance positivity.

It is too easy these days to be negative because there is so much that is going wrong in the world. Performative politics is rewarded with more likes, more coverage, and more reactions. Focusing on the negative or the controversial seems to be how you get attention on social media.

I am deliberate about not wasting my time on negativity. The politics of Texas or California? I don't live in either state. Do I wish they would do things the way I like? Yes. Can I influence it? Probably not. Should I waste my time focusing on it? No.

Reading and forwarding anything negative or disturbing social media is a misuse of my energy. Reading about bad events (natural disasters in another country or murders in some faraway place) only serves to drain me. It is not that I don't care, it is that I don't need to dwell. The person who is driving too slow or too fast on the highway does not need my anger. They need me to avoid them so we can both be safe.

When someone does something I don't understand why, I am trying to improve the way I react. One way to do that is apply the "Three Plausible, Kind Reasons" approach to any situation. The technique is fairly simple. If someone does something I don't like, I know my instantaneous negative reaction will happen, so I allow it. Then I immediately take charge of the situation and come up with three good reasons why the other person did what they did.

For example, one day I was running on a road with no sidewalks. There was another person walking on the other side of the road. Cars were coming in both directions of the road at the same time. We all could not fit in the road safely. The guy driving towards me did not slow down or move away from me, so I had to stop running and hop into someone's flower garden to be safe. After I got over my initial anger, I applied my new rule:

1. "Maybe he was late for a breakfast and was trying to get to his destination in a hurry."
2. "Perhaps he was distracted by something else that happened to him that day."

3. "It is possible he did not see me running or he thinks it is my job to get out of the street."

The idea of three reasons is actually fun. You may have to get creative. You put yourself in the other person's shoes or the shoes you are in when you are in a hurry, are unkind, etc. Let's face it, we all do things that others can construe as not great.

Three Plausible, Kind Reasons is about trying to avoid negativity. The flip side of the coin is to enhance positivity.

I am trying to embrace positivity by acknowledging and speaking to workers at grocery stores or restaurants. Simply engaging them in the same way as I would a neighbor may help lighten their day. Using their name (most places have name tags) allows me to acknowledge them directly. I have no idea if I made a difference in their day, but I am hopeful I do. A small connection can go a long way.

Rose is a more positive person than me. She believes people are good by nature and will do the right thing most of the time. She did not need to "Embrace Positive" like I needed to. She took a slightly different path, embracing "Whatever good we can do today" even more than before.

"After what happened in St. Croix, this comes back to me now with new meaning. Often, we find the volume of things that need our attention in our world to be overwhelming, Rose suggested. "It's easy to be discouraged and think that we can't make a difference. So why bother? My new perspective is *'Why not think about these few words: whatever good we can do today?'* The last word, "today", means more to me now. Dean and I learned very clearly that tomorrow is not promised. "

"Whatever good I can do today, is what I focus on."

#4 A New Purpose. Support St. Croix. Do good.

What are you "supposed" to do when a life-changing event comes along? What if you don't like being the center of attention? This event makes me "that guy". Being willing to talk about the event allows me to process it. It also allows others to hear the story. Perhaps simply talking about the ways I have been changed by this event will impact others Talking about The Hug, for instance, is hard for people to resist.

It took a while of contemplation to come up with something big. Rose and I knew we wanted to do something with this event to measurably help a larger community. The needs in this world are great. It is easy to get overwhelmed with ideas. In addition, our means are limited.

We decided creating a fund for the ongoing programming and maintenance of the Governor Juan F. Luis Hospital & Medical Center in St. Croix. The "why" answer is pretty easy. That hospital was integral to saving my life. What better way to honor and give back to them than through donations?

However, the story of why the need is so big is much deeper than that.

In September 2017, two Category 5 hurricanes struck the US Virgin Islands within a two-week period. First Hurricane Irma smashed into St. Croix, creating widespread damage. That was followed by Hurricane Maria, the deadliest hurricane in terms of category strength to strike the US Virgin Islands.

After both hurricanes, the office of VI Congresswoman Stacey Plaskett stated that 90% of buildings in the Virgin Islands were damaged or destroyed and 13,000 of those buildings had lost their roofs. The Governor Juan F. Luis Hospital & Medical Center on St. Croix suffered roof damage and flooding, but remained (barely) operational.

Six months after Irma, only 25% of residents of St. Croix had electricity. Many homes still had no roofs.

As for the Governor Juan F. Luis Hospital & Medical Center, the roof leaked, making the top (third) floor unusable. When I was at the hospital in November 2022 (five years later), the third floor still could not be occupied. The decision has been made in the interim to tear down the hospital in the future and build a new one.

The hospital will be rebuilt. But it will need funds to help maintain it and to improve its outreach. That is where we can all chip in. Rose and I are going to donate all of the profits from the sale of this book to the hospital's foundation. Thank you.

But you can go farther. Become a donor to our fund at www.TheLedgeBook.com or www.BelvoirPress.com. We can all make a difference to the place that saved me.

Epilogue: Make Moments Matter

"Wisdom happily lives with mystery, doubt, and unknowing." Richard Rohr, Falling Upwards

It is rewarding to have a purpose in life larger than myself. Rose and I, with the decision to donate the profits to the Governor Juan F. Luis Hospital and Medical Center in St. Croix, have new purpose.

As a buyer of this book, it makes you part of the dream. You can take it further if you would like. Pass the word onto friends, neighbors, co-workers, and family members to go to **www.TheLedgeBook.com** to get more information and donate to the hospital. All donations are tax deductible, thanks to the help of our friends at The Dayton Foundation. Our community can do good for people who desperately need it.

Rose was asked by a colleague, "What do you want people to do after reading this book? What action do you want them to take?"

"That's a hard one for me. I've spent the last 10 years trying to stop mothering, telling people what they should do or need to do," She reflected. "I guess I hope that our readers will have a renewed sense of hope about their lives and about the goodness of others, especially those who are different in some way."

"I hope that our readers will find more gratitude in their daily lives. Try adopting an attitude of being open to whatever moments they find in front of them. It can be as simple as being kind to the people you encounter each day. I know we can't say yes to everything asked of us, we'd be overwhelmed. But we can ask ourselves, perhaps prayerfully, *is this for me to do?"*

The two of us spent a lot of time together and apart thinking through how we could make our story matter, beyond being an interesting read and gathering donations for a worthy cause. We wanted to make this story more than that.

Author and professor Adam Grant provided inspiration and courage when he contrasted self-promotion (publicizing self) and idea promotion. He wrote, "Idea promotion is. . . *I made something I am really proud of. I hope is valuable to you. I hope you get some joy out of it.* If you don't put that idea out in the world, you're depriving people of benefitting from what you poured your heart into; that to me seems like a mistake."

Our idea is that we can all Make Moments Matter.

Moments are the daily events in our lives: thoughts, interactions, connections. We are all presented with numerous moments every day in our life. We get the choice to pay attention to those moments, pause, think, and then decide to be intentional about taking action. If we can do that a little more each day, we have the chance to make a difference in our lives and the lives of others.

The two of us understand now, more fully and gratefully, that moments are building blocks to a potentially more fulfilling life. How do you know if this moment might matter or not? You don't. However, there is much upside potential to being more aware of the moment. There is little risk to spending some time on it.

These moments in our life are going to all be different. Big and small. Consequential and minor. Noticeable and not. Increasing our awareness of more moments gives us the opportunity to make a difference.

Be attentive and act on moments when they are presented to you. Remember what Rose says, "I try to listen to what God is saying to me". Sometimes that will mean saying "yes" to a moment. Often it will mean taking responsibility for doing something. Say hello to that person you see on the street. When a friend or neighbor goes quiet, reach out. When you see someone in distress or in need, take responsibility to be a good person.

That is why I choose more often to open up to someone about what happened to me, even if it is someone I do not know well. Maybe I owe it to others to let them know good things happen to people. There are good people in the world willing to take risks to save a life. Maybe my story will inspire someone else or touch them in some way to act.

I've been given a gift. I nearly had my life taken away. I came out of it with as few injuries as anyone could expect. My physical recovery was measured in hours, not months. I got back to my daily life quickly.

I am much more intentional about doing the things that are important to me. Living each day understanding that this day is all I have. I get to compare what the Dean after November 22 does with what the Dean prior to November 22 would have done. I am a writer. How could I not share this story and its aftermath?

I've been asked the same question as Rose, "what do you want people to get out of this book?" I have three thoughts:

#1. Even when things feel hopeless, there is always hope.

#2. Be open to the idea that people are good at their core and will sacrifice for you in your time of need.

#3. Make Moments Matter. We are all presented with numerous moments every day in our life. Make a choice to pay attention to a few more moments to make a difference in your life and the life of others.

At this moment, you have the opportunity to become a donor to the St. Croix hospital. Or pass the name of this book onto a friend. Who knows what the downstream impact might be?

Be a donor to a worthy cause:

Gov. Juan F. Luis Hospital and Medical Center

www.TheLedgeBook.com

Click on the "Donate" Button

All donations will support the hospital. We have set up the RosaDean Foundation Fund #5112 as a component fund of The Dayton Foundation.

Appendix 1: Biographies

"Life is a more intense experience once we are no longer on autopilot",
Wendy Wood

It will never be possible to repay those people who saved my life in any way close to the debt we owe them. I know I had tears in my eyes when I met each of them, this time under far better circumstances. Meeting them in person and getting to know more of their story was a treasure. Our everlasting gratitude and love for them is the best we can do. We hope that the funds we are able to earn for the St. Croix Hospital is a long-lasting tribute to them.

The people to follow are a reminder that there are many unselfish people in this world. May we all never forget that.

The Rescuers (in order of appearance)

John and Amie Jarvie

John and Amie were on a cruise of the Caribbean. November 22, 2022 was their one day in St. Croix. Like me, Amie had done a lot of research and the tide pools were their top priority. They had plans to visit the tide pools and then take in as much of the island as they could in their single day.

Their availability of a phone to get the 911 call started almost immediately after I disappeared was the key first domino in the rescue. They were the right people at the right place.

Amie calls Massachusetts her home. John is originally from California. They now live in Utah. When they decided to get married, they pledged to take a honeymoon every month to somewhere fun. St. Croix was their November 2022 monthly honeymoon. It ended up being a memorable one.

Amie is a teacher of the deaf, a Listening Spoken Language specialist. She is also an Auditory verbal therapist working with kids (1–3-year-olds) and their families building their brains to learn to speak and read lips. John works and repairs bikes. They also spend a lot of time (when not traveling) helping in the development of their grandson, TJ, who has spent a lot of time fighting against the odds to survive. TJ and I were connected in our struggles over those few days.

Karl Fredrick

"King" Karl Frederick, the first person to get in contact with me after I was trapped in the small cavern, was in his role as a tour guide for Tan Tan Tours, where he had been working for 15 years. When we got together with him in June 2023, Karl was holding down four part-time jobs: Tour Guide, Construction Worker, Master Chef, and Island Escort. He knows an unbelievable amount about the native fruits and vegetables on St. Croix. He can tell you how to choose the tastiest ones and how to cook them properly.

Born in St. Croix, he has lived most of his life there. He took a detour for a few years as a master chef in Kennebunkport, Maine at the White Barn Inn and Resort preparing food for the wealthy and famous guests. The cold weather eventually drove him back to St. Croix.

While most of Karl's family moved off the island after the closing of the large refinery in 2012, he stayed behind to be with his grandmother, who he characterized as the most important person in his world. He knows so much about the history of the island and tells it with a passion.

Not content with staying being static, he is studying to be a pilot. He wants to fly private jets because he has a desire to be connected to the people he serves.

Devron Smith

Devron was also in his role as a tour guide for Tan Tan Tours that fateful day. He went with Karl on the rocks to find me. In an incredible coincidence, Devron was the tour guide for some friends of ours when they went to St. Croix for their honeymoon in 2021. I only found that out through research on the Tan Tan website where I saw a review by my friend. Devron and his wife have two young children.

Ben Torkelson

If not for Ben's preparedness, I don't know if I would have survived. He is the one who decided to put his rescue rope in his jeep for the first time in a year. He also was the only person to bring an oxygen tank. That tank provided me with much-needed oxygen for those three hours we were on the rocks waiting for the helicopter rescue. Without it, who knows what would have happened.

I think back to Ben's statement about the rescue rope quite a lot. "I have not carried my rescue rope with me for over a year. I think I will throw it in my truck today." Little did he know how important that would be on this day. What would have happened if he had decided, like he had done every day for the past year and NOT included his rope? Things would have been much different.

What are the odds that a trained rescue operative, with a jeep full of the equipment needed to perform a rescue and take care of a person rescued, is "in the neighborhood"? If Ben had been at home, it would have added at least 45 more minutes of prep and drive time. I might not have lasted that much longer.

Ben is originally from Washington state. He served in the Marines for five years and was a civilian working with the Army for a few years after that, including time in Iraq. He has served as a chaplain, is a St. Croix Rescue volunteer, where he does a lot of medical work. Ben is also a Coast Guard Auxiliary member. The Auxiliary is the civilian uniformed volunteer component of the United States Coast Guard that works alongside the Guard in safety and rescue. He is also a PADI licensed Master Scuba Diver.

He and his wife, Stephanie, have three children. They moved to St. Croix in March 2021. They were looking to 'try something new'. They visited St. Croix and fell in love with it. While they were visiting, they got an offer to sell their house in Washington and decided to move.

Jason Henry

Jason wears so many hats. He is Director of Communicable Disease for St. Croix, a Rescue St. Croix Volunteer, and an AeroMD Special Ops

Coordinator. One of four St. Croix Rescue volunteers, a group that appears at nearly every mission. We heard stories about them firefighting, rescuing, providing safety for traffic accidents, and supporting police and EMTs on all manner of injuries and crimes. It is a daily role, not an occasional one.

He has lived in Antigua, England, St. Thomas, and St. Croix. On top of all of that, he is building his house. He and his wife have seven children.

Malik Garvey

Malik was born and raised in St. Croix. He has spent a good part of his life on the island, but was away for 15 years in Dallas, Texas as a security officer at a refinery. He got a call in early 2019 asking if he would like to learn to be a fire fighter in St. Croix. He decided to return. He is a firefighter and ambulance driver now. He completed his Emergency medical responder certification in September 2022 (two months before the incident). He is also working on his EMT certification.

November 22 was his first day as an ambulance driver. He told me he has found his niche in life, to be a rescue responder. He also gave me his St. Croix Rescue shirt, which I proudly wear as a reminder of the rescue squad.

The Helicopter Crew

Lieutenant William "Travis" Cox

Lt. Cox was the pilot in command (PIC) for the helicopter. He comes from a Navy family (father, grandfather and great-grandfather). Born in Groton, CT, his family moved with the navy. He graduated from high school in Nevada and college from the University of North Florida. Most of his family now lives in Alabama.

After college, he entered the US Marine Corp in 2007 and achieved his wings in 2010. He supported Operation Enduring Freedom, serving in Afghanistan twice. In 2017, he joined the US Coast Guard and was transferred to US Coast Guard Air Station Borinquen in 2019. We were lucky that he was still there, as most people rotate every 3-4 years to another assignment. He met his wonderful wife, Kristin, in college and they have three amazing young boys, Wyatt, Rory and Everett.

As the Pilot in Command (PIC), he conducts the crew briefing, performs exterior and interior inspections of the helicopter, and plans the mission. He is responsible for all phases of flying the aircraft, along with the safety of the crew and passengers.

Lieutenant JG William "Billy" Boardman

Billy Boardman was the co-pilot (CP) and the pilot monitor (PM). He is originally from Woodstock, Georgia. He graduated from the U.S. Coast Guard Academy in 2019. After earning his wings, he was assigned to Borinquen in May 2022.

As the Copilot (CP) he assists the pilot on all the flight responsibilities as well as assisting the flight mechanic in determining the cargo and passenger distribution and computing the Center of Gravity (CG) of the helicopter.

As the PM, he handles any cockpit duty that may potentially distract the pilot from concentrating on flight control operation. One example is chief communication officer, allowing the pilot to fly the helicopter. He monitored and maintained numerous channels open with rescuers, Coast Guard Command Center, Coast Guard Boats, and the crew.

Beau James, Jr

Beau James is originally from Baltimore, Maryland and went to high school in Williamsburg, Virginia. His dad (for 30+ years) and his brother are both in the Coast Guard. He completed Coast Guard Boot Camp in Cape May, NJ in 2015. His initial assignment out of boot camp was the Coast Guard Honor Guard in Washington, DC for two and a half years.

He then completed Aviation Maintenance Technician (AMT) "A School" where he learned the basics of being an AMT. He was deployed to Astoria, Oregon for three years. From there he volunteered to be part of the Air Station Borinquen airframe transition in Aguadilla, Puerto Rico. In December of 2021 he completed his qualification as a MH-60T Flight Mechanic, meaning he could also be deployed on helicopter missions in addition to maintaining the fleet of helicopters.

When he is not flying, he works on a team that maintains all of the Coast Guard Helicopters in San Juan. On flights, he has a variety of roles.

AST3 Curren Hinote

Curren is a native of Jacksonville, Florida and also comes from a navy family. Out of high school, he "wanted to be part of something bigger and better". He joined the Coast Guard in 2018 and graduated from swimmer school in 2019. While his role is commonly referred to as "rescue swimmer", he does a lot more than that. He is responsible for the maintenance of all of the survival gear (Stokes Basket, first aid, etc.). He is the one who gets lowered down onto the scene and is expected to make the decision on how the extraction is to be conducted. San Juan is his first deployment.

The Command Center (911 call)

CWO3/OSS3 Daniel Capestany

CWO3 Daniel Capestany is a Command Center Command Duty Officer in the US Coast Guard (USCG) Sector San Juan Command Center. In this role, his team manages all of the 911 calls, all distress reports, as well as decisions on deployment of assets (ships, helicopter, personnel) in the execution of all Coast Guard Missions in Puerto Rico and the US Virgin Islands. He and his team were the ones receiving the original and all subsequent 911 call on my situation. He spent part of the time talking on the phone with Rose, gathering information.

He has been with the US Coast Guard for 22 years, 11 of which have been at the Sector San Juan Command Center. He was born and raised in Ponce, Puerto Rico.

This is his third tour at USCG Sector San Juan. His 1st tour was from November 2002 to May2007 and his second tour was from May 2010 to May2016. He is assigned to USCG Sector San Juan until 2026.

The Health Care Workers

Cadira McIntosh

Cadira is from St. Croix and was my ED nurse. We were told others characterize her as a positive, warm, people-oriented person. She was selected as the 2023 Governor Juan Luis Hospital Nurse of the Year for her service. She is married to an EMT in St. Croix.

Dr. Lauren Bacon

Dr. Bacon was my principal ED doctor. She is originally from the Los Angeles area and got her MD degree at Howard University in Washington DC. She went back to Southern California for her residency. Since 2023, she is studying at the University of Connecticut doing her International Disaster Medicine Fellowship. That means she is on call at any time to be deployed for disaster relief (manmade and natural – fires, hurricanes, etc.), refugee work, and NGO work. She told me she has a "go" bag at home, knowing she could be called at any time to take off within 24 hours for a place needing her help.

Her story of how she decided to become a doctor was very moving. She told me, "I witnessed a mass casualty event when I was a teenager. Growing up in LA, there was an 86-year-old man who (accidently) drove through the Santa Monica Farmers Market and ran over people (That was July 16, 2003 and it ended up with 10 people dead and 70 injured). It was my first-time seeing injuries and dead babies and women. I was 14. That stuck with me. I knew I had a greater purpose. At 14, I could not do something. In the future, I knew I wanted to be in a position where I knew how can I be of service. In addition, my father was sick a lot. He had every medical condition you could think of. He was my medical text book."

So far in her young career, she has been deployed to Ethiopia, Haiti, Ecuador, Costa Rica, and St. Croix. There will be many more for this giving person.

Amanda Crossland

Amanda was my ED respiratory therapist. Given the bad state of my lungs and my breathing, Amanda spent a lot of time working with me. Her role was critical in making sure my breathing was improved and that I did not suffer from secondary drowning.

She is originally from Oklahoma. She told me that she "worked through the whole COVID pandemic and was in a bad space. A friend of mine was down in St. Croix and told me it was different. I came down to St. Croix on August 11, 2021. I plan on staying." She is selling her house in the States and moving to St. Croix.

Amanda is a third-generation respiratory therapist, preceded by her mom and grandmother.

Steve Chmura

Steve was an ED nurse who was temporarily assigned to the ICU for a couple weeks while someone else was out. That movement was a blessing, and another one of the small miracles. Steve was my daytime ICU nurse (7:00 am – 7:00 pm) on Wednesday, my first day in ICU. He was there the day I showed the most drastic improvement.

Steve grew up in Michigan owning several businesses before transitioning to a nurse spending many years in Alaska as an ICU, ED and Flight nurse. He and his wife Amy, moved aboard a sailboat and filled a need for nursing in. St Croix.

Steve and Amy have since started their own business. They saw that St. Croix had no recycling facility and formed their own company recycling plastic to make furniture and a wide variety of items. Their goal is to help the US Virgin Islands reduce waste and provide local jobs. They are hopeful that the business will prove profitable enough for them to fund a program similar to one they were part of in Alaska by providing medical training to healthcare volunteers and professionals in remote regions of the world.

Amber Wyse

Amber was my Wednesday night, Thursday morning (until 7:00 a.m.) ICU nurse. She had the distinction of being the one who gave me the pot of tea that I could drink. We shared a laugh together after we met again in person, because that was the most momentous event of our time together.

Amber is originally from Memphis, Tennessee. She had a nursing assignment in New Orleans during the COVID pandemic that she said was rough. She came to St. Croix in 2021, not sure if she wanted to continue nursing. Luckily, she was there at the hospital when I needed her.

Amber has subsequently bought an 18-foot boat because she likes to go fishing in the sea. She is out of nursing and holding two jobs: bartender at the Hotel on Protestant Cay, the most popular beach in Christiansted and working on a charter fishing boat. Her joy was palpable when we met. She felt much more relaxed and was doing things she loved: serving people and fishing. It was so kind of her to spend her birthday morning at breakfast with Rose and I on June 12.

One thing I will always remember from sitting with her at breakfast when we returned in June 2023 was her connection to the people. As we eat, she waved and talked with a variety of people. These were not people she worked with, nor were they her neighbors. They were part of the people who worked near the boardwalk like she does. She said, "I may not know their names, but I know if I needed help, they would help me." She was part of a friendly community that took care of each other.

Kristen Lee

Kristen was my ICU nurse during the day on Thursday (Thanksgiving) and Friday (release from hospital day). She had one of the toughest jobs in dealing with me. I desperately wanted to leave the hospital and be with my family on Thanksgiving. The only one who could possibly make that happen was the doctor, but he never came to see me. Kristen had to listen to me complain and get angry, not at her expense. She tried to advocate for me while also trying to listen to me.

We had a great time talking about a mutual interest in hiking. She had gone on a pilgrimage hike in Spain called the Camino de Santiago.

Kristen is originally from Southern California. She came to St. Croix in 2021. She has now moved to the Island permanently, having found a significant other, enjoying the people and all that the island offers.

Grace Kim

Grace Kim was my respiratory therapist in the ICU. At the time, she has been a respiratory therapist for 10 years. Originally from Tucson, Arizona, she also went to college there. She had never ventured out of Arizona until she got done with school. She told me: "I had a map on the wall and decided to throw a dart at it. Wherever it lands, as long as it was in the US, I would go there. It landed on St. Thomas, US Virgin Islands. I had never heard of it, so I did some research. I found it had a facility, packed up all my things, sold what I did not need, and moved to St. Thomas. At the time, St. Thomas was not hiring, so I reached out the hospital in St. Croix and was hired there."

She was at St. Croix the first time from 2016 through Category 5 Hurricane Maria in September 2017. She met her husband at another island, St. Thomas. They lost everything due to Maria and needed to start over again. They moved to Saipan, a more remote island, the largest of the Northern Mariana Islands, a US Commonwealth in the Western Pacific with a population of 43,000. After that she worked at a hospital in Key West, Florida for a couple years.

She and her husband decided to move back to St. Croix, where they now live and work.

Emergency Department

One of the unfortunate things about the events of the ER is that, despite being there for nearly 10 hours, it is impossible to remember all of the caregivers. I feel badly that I cannot acknowledge each of them. I know that Dr Beth Joseph, Dr. Lacey Menkensmith, and Nurse Tim were part of my care team.

Their efforts are all part of a long chain of events that led to my survival. I think this probably provides some insight into the type of individual that works in an ED. They never know what they are going to see. They won't know what condition the patient will be in, so they need to be flexible. There is a good possibility they will never get recognition for the success of the patient (as with me, since ICU was the place that I emerged from). These are intrinsically motivated people. It is humbling to recognize they worked to save me yet knew they might never get any credit for saving a life. This book is a small token of payback.

A few others to acknowledge

I spent months trying every way I could think of to find the people acknowledged above. In some cases, my son, Stephen, had the foresight to ask people their names and cell phone numbers. Without his work that day, under all of that strain, we would not have been able to connect with so many people.

From there, I did searches on social media (LinkedIn and Facebook), on Coast Guard websites, and the Hospital website. Some were helpful and some led nowhere.

I want to acknowledge a few people, without whom I would have never been able to connect with so many of the people who were important in saving my life.

First is Doug Koch, the CEO of the Gov. Juan F. Luis Hospital and Medical Center in St. Croix. I was getting nowhere trying to find out information on people who served me at the hospital. In desperation, I searched on LinkedIn for people who worked at the hospital. Doug's profile was the first search result and he was open to messages. I reached out to him with a request to talk and a link to my blog post.

Doug responded that night. He wrote in part: "Dean, first and foremost, thank God you are alive. How often do we all see random messages from strangers and ignore them? I am so happy that I did not do that tonight. I have read your rescue blog and found myself holding my breath and cannot imagine the experience and emotions that you, your family and the rescuers went through." Thus began the wheels of connection. Doug connected me with his communications team.

James "Jay" Rollins and Aniah John became my "pen pals" as I explained my wishes and began the process for coming to visit the hospital in person in June 2023. They were invaluable in setting up my day at the hospital to visit the nurses and to get a copy of my medical records. Two unbelievable busy people were generous with their time.

At the coast Guard in San Juan, Puerto Rico, Ricardo Castrodad was my contact. Another one-man-band trying to do all of the public affairs for the base, he was most accommodating. The opportunity to see the helicopter crew, meet members of the Coast Guard boats, and the Command Center were all part of the day Ricardo put together. His dedication and generosity reflect well on the Coast Guard. He was a fantastic host and made Rose and I full-time Coast Guard advocates.

It takes a lot of support to pull a book, the website, and marketing together. Thanks to our kids for help: Courtney, the "Marketing Intern" and sounding board for a bunch of ideas. Stephen for help with Pricing, Finance, and Fulfillment. Nate for being the final proofreader and editor which added so much to the book. Our discussion led to a significant improvement in the flow of the book. Luke for being the creative one who came up with the title for the book.

We appreciate our "marketing team": Megan, Cassy, Kelly, Joan, Beth, Bob, and Brian for helping us get the word out in so many places. Shoutouts to Rose L and Jane for providing perspectives on an early draft of this book that helped steer it in a better direction. Thanks to Brian and Heather at MartinInk for their editorial guidance on how to put a complex story together in a concise, exciting manner. Your feedback took this book to another level. The Book Trailer, masterfully created by Terry at TriLevel Records.com, exceeded our dreams.

Appendix 2: The Return

"This awful catastrophe is not the end but the beginning. History does no end so. It is the way its chapters open". St. Augustine

How does one thank someone else for helping save their life? It seems like such a challenge. To be honest, Rose and I found it to be very simple. Give people big hugs and be present. Seeing Rose and I was a profound experience for many of the people we saw on our trip. Not because it was "us", but for what we represented. A win. A success. Why they do the job they do. Sometimes the sense of touch can be a very strong connection. We felt it with so many people.

Our trip to Puerto Rico and St. Croix in June 2023 was more than we could have expected.

A colleague of Rose's had shown her small stones she got for clients with "thank you" on them. She said no one wanted them. Rose took them thinking how much she had to be thankful for. A few weeks before our trip, she came up with the idea to give them to the rescuers. She got a gold paint marker and wrote, "Dean and Rose, 11/22/22" on the back of each one. We both thought it might be a great way to thank people and remind them of that momentous day.

Rose still had some trepidation about the trip. She thought, "I couldn't help but wonder how it would feel to make a trip like this. I had no similar experiences. I hoped for the best, having faith in the two of us to handle whatever happened together. There was some relief when the trip was finally here. No more to be anxious about. Just go do me."

Some people thought Rose and I going back to the Annaly Bay tide pools was "brave". It must have been "hard to do". I am getting better at not simply dismissing other's observations, whether I agree or not. If they think it is "brave", I need to honor their thinking and not dismiss it. I do not think it was particularly brave to go.

I needed to get some closure. I wanted to be able to face ocean water without fear. I wanted St. Croix to be a magical, beautiful place, not a place I would forever associate with fear and death.

Now that we planned to go, I needed help to make connections with people. The helicopter crew was in Aguadilla, Puerto Rico (a two-hour drive west of San Juan, Puerto Rico). The Coast Guard Command Center and some of the Coast Guard boats were in San Juan. The rescuers and the hospital were in St. Croix, about 45 minutes away by flight. Through persistence, and with the help of Ricardo Castrodad of the US Coast Guard and Jay Rollins of the Gov. Juan F. Luis Hospital in St. Croix, we had a full agenda.

First stop was Puerto Rico, home to the helicopter crew and the Command Center.

We arrived in San Juan on Tuesday, June 6th. That night, the two of us enjoyed dinner and walked to a nearby beach in the evening. That felt normal and good.

In the morning we drove to Aguadilla, home to the Coast Guard helicopter base. We were met by the helicopter pilot, Travis Cox. He took us to a conference room where we met the rest of the crew. It was very helpful that they had their logs of events and timelines. We could get a much more detailed and accurate understanding of what they did and why they did it. Now we knew why they made all of those passes, different than what Rose and Stephen had expected.

They had all participated in previous rescues but had never met a person they rescued later and been thanked. It clearly meant a lot to them that we were there to thank them. This gift of the thank you stones was appreciated. They gave us an in-depth tour of the base. They were so kind to us.

"We will be celebrating 40 years of marriage in August. And we get to do that because of you," Rose told them. "Thank you from the bottom of my heart."

* * * *

Meeting every person was special in its own way. Two stories convey some of the profoundness of the week.

The US Coast Guard Command Center in San Juan, Puerto Rico is sometimes referred to the "911 Center". After meeting the personnel and talking with them, we learned their role is much bigger than that. The initial 911 calls come to them. Beyond that, they have to make decisions on what assets to deploy (air, watercraft, ambulance, etc.) for each situation. That deployment decision is critical and must be made in a timely manner. If they are too quick to deploy resources, those resources may not be available for a truly critical incident that comes up later. Waiting too long may cost lives.

They also need to coordinate with a wide variety of resources outside the Coast Guard. For example, they needed to make sure an ambulance was ready for me immediately when the helicopter dropped me off at the St. Croix airport.

The Command Center personnel have a life-in-the-balance job. In my case, sending one of two available helicopters on a one-hour flight southeast to be involved in a rescue meant the rest of their vast area of water they patrol was without one of its key assets. It is not an easy job. High stress with people's lives in the balance.

The Command Center is a secure location (restricted entry, must be escorted, no phones, locked doors), so very few people are afforded the opportunity to visit. The people who work there don't get many visitors. Rose and I had the opportunity to tell them in person the larger story of how I became trapped, how I was rescues, and the recovery.

Other than the person or two who was manning the phones, the rest of the team got to hear the story and ask questions. The energy in the room was transcendent. You could feel that they were moved by the story. More importantly, they got to hear our gratitude in person. They are on the front end of many calls every day, but never at the back end to get the full story. The energy (the aura) in that room is something I will never forget.

The second story is the trip back to the tide pools after we had been in St. Croix for a couple days. Karl Frederick, the first person to make contact with me as I was in the cave, took us on a personal trip to the pools. He stopped the jeep a few times on the way to the pools to tell us what he was thinking and what he has gone through since the day of my rescue. Clearly a spiritual man, the rescue was a seminal event for him. However, he never had the chance to process the event and get some of the help Rose and I got. He still had a lot of anxiety about the day's events. Imagine being a hero and then struggling with it all. We hope that our presence was a part of his healing.

Surprisingly, going back to the tide pools was not nearly as traumatic as I anticipated. I was not scared or anxious. It had the feeling of a "field trip", visiting an important place. Perhaps it was because the few days spent in Puerto Rico and St. Croix prior to the tour took some of the sharp emotional edges off. We had experienced a lot of grateful emotions by then. Another reason was that the water levels were significantly less than November 22, so the danger seemed much smaller. The waves were incredibly calmer. Karl was vigilant, nonetheless.

Rose's original plan was to not get in the water at all. Not even the first tidal pool. She started to avoid the water and Karl said no. He instructed her to go through the pool because it was safer than climbing on the rocks. His experience was those slippery, sharp rocks were dangerous. Rose's experience was the water in the tide pools was not safe.

She remembers being unhappy with the instructions, but she listened to Karl. "I wanted to feel grounded. That's hard to do when you're swimming, as I had to in some part of the first tide pool. As we climbed over the wall to see the second tidal pool, I was mentally bracing myself."

It was amazing how much calmer the ocean was. The depth of the water in the tide pool was multiple feet lower than last year. There were no waves crashing over the wall. We learned that Rose, Stephen, and I picked a freakishly bad day on November 22 to be at the pools. There is no way we could know that back then.

Rose has a much more vivid memory of that tide pool than I did. Her apprehension was noticeable and understandable. Upon seeing the tide pool her reaction was surprise. As she recollected, "We look at tide pool #2 and it looks like it had been drained. The hole is right there in plain view. It is bigger than the volleyball-sized hole mostly filled with water that I had in my mind since November 22. The water level throughout the pool is under the lip of the hole by at least 18 inches."

"I did not expect my first reaction to be I felt totally safe. Looking down, I thought yikes, the hole is huge compared to what I remember."

Rose and I were able to sit on the ocean floor right next to the hole I went down. It was a surreal experience. The place that was a death trap on November 22 was now a hole in the rocks with little water going into it. It was not a scary place at all.

Seeing the tide pool and reliving that day was part of my healing. Now I know that my mishap on November 22, 2022 was simply one of life's random acts. We were not foolhardy that day. We didn't take unnecessary risks to get a picture. We were in the wrong place at the wrong moment in time.

"My emotions are very mixed up. I'm angry that I can't get a picture of this place the way it looked that day," Rose continued. "At the same time, I'm glad I can see all this so clearly. I can also see that the wall I was standing on has an upper and lower part. I must have been standing on the lower part or I couldn't have helped Stephen that day. I don't remember any waves crashing over the wall that day. I believe they would have knocked me off the wall. Now I see I was protected from any waves by the upper portion of the wall. I watched Dean and Karl talk through the events of 11/22/22. I hoped it was as therapeutic for Karl as it was us."

Each of us has different perspectives on the tide pool and the hole. For me, it was the place I went down the hole. For Rose, it was an extremely emotional place. It was the place she saw her husband die in. For Karl, it was a place where he connected on a deeply spiritual level with me that drained him of his energy.

Our time with Karl allowed us to get to know him better as a person. He is a fascinating person with a variety of interests. Once we got away from the pools, where he was clearly trying to be very protective of us, he wanted to share the beauty of St. Croix. He took us around to different parts of the island and described the plants and the terrain. He became more three dimensional to me, more than just a hero, but a person with varied knowledge and interests. We made a connection at another level.

* * * *

Before meeting with Karl, we arrived in St. Croix and went immediately to the hospital. We met some of the nurses who took care of me. Meeting the hospital people was a different experience. They were all busy. We met with each of them one at a time. We had four individual meetings set up, spread out over the next couple days.

"I had a clutching in my stomach as we approached St. Croix," Rose remembers. "I find it's best to just acknowledge those feelings as valid and just breath through it. What were the next few days to hold?"

"In the evening, we met with Dean's ED nurse, Cadira. This was a most emotional meeting for me," Rose recalled. "I remembered Cadira very well. She was a calm in the storm of that time in the ED. Her manner was straight forward, caring and low key."

"I remembered back to that day and her noticing Stephen's scraped and bleeding legs. Though he wasn't a patient and she didn't have time to care for him, she got out supplies for him to take care of himself. The beauty of her service left an indelible impression on me. She simply responded to everything Dean, we, and the doctors needed that night. It was moving to meet her in a much less stressful situation."

I had a similar emotional experience when we met Kristen, my nurse on Thursday and on Friday, which were the last days I was in the hospital. Since I was feeling much better on those days, the two of us had a chance to connect. I spent a lot of time talking with her in the hospital.

Rose watched the two of us talk, and was touched that Kristen remembered some of the things we had talked about. From Rose's perspective, "I know Dean choked up when he had to say goodbye to Kristen. It was his first health care worker to meet on our trip and I believe the enormity of the situation came to the front for him."

* * * *

On our trip, we got to meet these amazing people: all four helicopter crew members; the two people that Rose spoke to directly on the 911 call; four of the five nurses who primarily took care of me, and four of the six rescuers. It was fantastic to talk with each of them. All were gracious with their time. All had stories they remembered for my care or meeting the family. It was like a reunion with long-lost friends.

We now realize we profoundly made each person's day by returning to visit them. None of them typically get to see the "end of the story". They all know pieces. To witness the real human that each of them helped save was something I did not realize would be so important. In their lives, they usually have to move on to the next day, the next rescue, the next emergency call, the next patient. Their work is never done. It is hard to remember individual cases. Until we help them remember they were part of a miraculous success, it all might blend together.

I was reminded of this quote by author and podcaster Shelby Stanger: "When you finish your epic adventure, even if it's small, give yourself grace at the finish line and try to celebrate along the way." I celebrate each day, especially when I tell someone else how special the trip was.

Appendix 3: Why Did This Happen?

I had one additional question that stuck with me from the start.

What if I turned this question:

From: Why did this happen **to me**?

To: Why did this happen?

That was my initial reaction to this whole ordeal. I was trying to take the spotlight off myself and put it on others. It was a natural reaction. Thanking others is good. Maybe just as important, if this was about others, that means it was not about me very much. I came to realize that if I ducked some of the story, it would be easier. On me.

Could I concoct a story that said this incident happened for the benefit of others?

As I pondered it more, this event was not just about me. While I was the center of the story, multiple lives were impacted directly. Just like me, all the rescuers and health care workers were caught up in events that put them in a particular place and time. Their future lives were going to be impacted by the things that happened that day.

Might it be possible that one of the members of the rescue group was wondering about their purpose in life? Maybe they were going through a hard time. It is rare for most of us to have an opportunity to directly impact the survival of another person, particularly a stranger. How might the impact of this event weigh on their views about the fragility of life? They can always turn back to this time and know they made a difference in a life. Is that something they think about?

Might this have been the first time any of them had directly saved a life? Seeing how distraught my wife and son were, and then being able to deliver the good news must have been life-changing for them. The opportunity to meet the rest of the family later that week (as well as me) hopefully brought home the importance of what they all did that day. Their life had meaning.

We don't know how it might have impacted any of the rescuers' lives now and in the future. Much like me, they had a day that was an inflection point, a time of significant change or a turning point in their lives. Sometimes we all need a reminder of how important family and friends are in our life. We take things for granted through the busyness of life. Perhaps they were neglecting their family in some way. This might have been a reminder to them of how important family is.

The healthcare workers deal with sick and injured patients every day.

I was the patient that lived. Maybe they needed that affirmation that day. Not every patient is going to get better. I imagine it is very hard to be in a role where life and death are sometimes so close. Perhaps one more piece of the "Why did this happen" was so that one of the healthcare workers could know that their work does save lives.

Perhaps it was for my family. We are a close family, and enjoy our time together. The St. Croix trip was planned because we rarely have the time to get all of us together, other than Christmas. Rose and I wanted to make a special time.

I remember asking Courtney about her feelings when she saw me in the hospital, especially Wednesday afternoon as I rapidly got better. She said, 'I knew my Dad was going to get better. I knew he would not be leaving us.' Since none of us has faced serious health issues, and we take pretty good care of ourselves, we assume we will always be there for each other.

It took me many months to recognize I could not hide from this story. The rescuers, the healthcare workers and I were tied. We are a family. There is no "me" and "them". Once I got to that place of intimate connection, it became so much easier to move forward. Now I could look at how this event impacted them as a way to understand them better, not as a way to hide from myself.

Appendix 4: Timeline

This is a reconstruction of the timeline of events of November 22, 2022. Some of the times provided by the US Coast Guard. Those designated "est." are estimates.

Time	Action
11:41 AM	Low tide; Dean, Rose, and Stephen arrive at Annaly Bay Tide Pools
12:25 est.	I am sucked into the small cavern
12:35 PM	Initial notification of a missing person to U.S. Coast Guard Command Center (911)
12:38	911 operator gathers information from Rose
12:40	Urgent Marine Information Broadcast; notification to all mariners in the area to provide assistance
12:40 (est.)	Rose, Stephen, John, and Amie arrive back at the beach, safe from the rocks
12:50	U.S. Coast Guard (USCG) small boat deployed
12:55 est.	Tan Tan Tours arrive at the beach
12:59	USCG Boat Forces Detachment St. Croix deployed
1:05 est.	Karl Frederick makes contact with me
1:06 est.	Devron comes back to the beach to tell them I am alive and Karl is talking to me
1:07	USCG Command Center notified I have been discovered. Mission changed from recovery to a rescue
1:15 est.	Ben Torkelson arrives on the scene and is informed it is now a rescue; rope needed
1:24	USCG small boat arrives on scene
1:25 est.	Ben tosses the rope down the hole and I receive it
1:30 est.	I am pulled out of the hole by Karl, Devron, and Ben
1:40 est.	Jason, Malik, and Bailey arrive.
1:46	Command Center notified I have been pulled out of the hole and am on the rocks
1:50 est.	The six rescuers and I move to a safer spot on the rocks.
2:07	Order is given to launch the helicopter
2:21	Command Center coordinates to get EMS; Tell them to deploy to airport to rendezvous with helicopter
2:28	Helicopter departs Puerto Rico

2:33	Helicopter checks in with Command Center
3:20	Helicopter is on scene in St. Croix
3:46	Helicopter deploys rescue swimmer (Curren) to the rocks to meet with rescuers
4:19	I and rescue swimmer are in the helicopter
4:27	Helicopter arrives at St. Croix airport
5:15	I am in the ER being initially evaluated